Family Ties
Don't Have to Bind

Family Ties Don't Have to Bind

Dr. James Osterhaus
with James Denney

Thomas Nelson Publishers
NASHVILLE • LONDON • VANCOUVER • ATLANTA

Published in Nashville, Tennessee, by Thomas Nelson, Inc., Publishers, and distributed in Canada by Word Communications, Ltd., Richmond, British Columbia, and in the United Kingdom by Word (UK), Ltd., Milton Keynes, England.

Names, places, and events in this book have been altered in order to protect the privacy of the individuals involved. Any case examples presented are fictional composites based on the authors' clinical experience with thousands of clients through the years. Any resemblance between these fictional characters and actual persons is coincidental.

Library of Congress Cataloging-in-Publication Data

Osterhaus, James P.
    "Family Ties Don't Have to Bind" / by James Osterhaus with James Denney.
        p.   cm.
    ISBN 0-8407-7805-8
    1. Parent and adult child.   I. Denney, James D.   II. Title.
HQ755.86.O88   1994
306.874—dc20   93–37373
                                                          CIP

Printed in the United States of America
1 2 3 4 5 6 7 — 98 97 96 95 94

To Mom and Dad,
who were always
easy to honor.

Contents

Family Ties
Don't Have to Bind

1

Honor Your Father and Your Mother

She put her hand on the phone, hesitating. It rang three more times under her fingers while the knot in her stomach tightened. She knew who was calling. He called every day at this time. What if she just didn't answer it? But of course, she had to answer it. What choice did she have? She lifted the receiver to her lips. "Hello?" she said weakly.

"Sandra, this is your father."

"Hi, Dad." She tried to put a cheerful lilt into her voice, but it fell flat.

"I thought you might want to know," her father said in a tone as caustic as Drano, "that your mother spent the night in the hospital."

"Her heart again?"

"Of course, her heart. She's a very sick woman, and the way you treat her, Sandra, I wonder how long we'll have her with us."

Sandra winced. She had heard that line many times before—and it always worked. She was sure her mother's heart was as strong, stubborn, and cantankerous as the rest of her, yet her father's accusation that she was killing her own mother never failed to find its target.

"Is Mom still in the hospital?" she asked. "What did the doctors say?"

"They released her this morning. You know doctors. They don't know anything. They couldn't find anything wrong with her, so they said it was probably indigestion. But your mother knows the difference between her heart and her stomach. Anyway, since you were too busy to help your mother yesterday, are you coming today? I hope you won't let her down again."

"Dad, I wasn't too busy yesterday," said Sandra. "I was sick. I had the flu. I didn't want to give it to Mom, and that's why I didn't come do her hair on the regular day."

"I never heard of anyone catching a cold from a shampoo and set."

"Not a cold, Dad, the flu," she said, sighing. "Okay, tell Mom I'll be right over. And tell her I'm sorry she's not feeling well."

"Get over here and tell her yourself." *Click.*

Sandra sighed and set down the receiver, waiting for the knot in her stomach to loosen. It didn't. Finally, she went into the kitchen and fixed a snack for her two boys, ages fourteen and eleven, and brought it to them in the den where they were playing Nintendo. "I'm going to Grandma and Grandpa's," she said, setting a plate of chips and dip between her sons. "Uh-huh," they murmured, never taking their eyes off the moving images on the TV screen. Sandra put on her coat, went out to the car, and drove away.

As she drove, she thought of all the things she wished she had said to her father on the phone. She could have said, "Mom *always* pulls these phony heart attacks, Dad. It's a family tradition. Grandma's in her eighties, and she's had a 'heart attack' at least twice a week for as long as I can remember. And Great-Grandma had these 'heart attacks' whenever things didn't go her way—and she lived to be ninety-six! Don't you think it's amazing, Dad, that people in Mom's family always have such bad hearts, yet they seem to live forever?" Oh, how she wished she could say *that* to her father!

Or how about this: "Dad, I'm forty-two years old, my husband's dead, I've got two children to raise, my house is a mess, I'm sick, I'm tired, and I've got my own life to live. Why don't you and Mom just bug off and get a life of your own?" She could just hear the fuming and sputtering on the other end! She savored the fantasy of finally telling her parents off, of finally declaring her independence at the age of forty-two. But that was all it was: a fantasy. She could no more say anything to hurt them than she could sprout wings and fly to the moon.

Sandra was a good daughter, and she always did what her parents told her.

"YOU'RE KILLING YOUR MOTHER"

Sandra was an only child, and she had lived almost all her life within a few minutes of the house where she had grown up in Alexandria, Virginia. She had spoken with her parents, by phone or in person, every single day of her life. Every Saturday, she went to their house and set her mother's hair, cleaned the bathrooms, vacuumed, and dusted—in short, all the jobs she never had time for in her own house. Her parents had always centered their lives around their only daughter, and they expected her to meet their needs and even anticipate their thoughts and whims.

Shortly after her husband died of cancer, Sandra moved to Virginia Beach. A friend from her high school days had offered her a job there, and Sandra leaped at the chance to start life over and find some independence. At first, the change of scenery seemed to help her find peace after the loss of her husband—but it didn't last long. Every day, her father phoned her and said, "You're killing your mother by moving so far away. After everything we've done to raise you right, I just don't see how you can be so ungrateful." Eventually, Sandra surrendered and moved with her two boys back to Alexandria.

When she came to see me for therapy, Sandra was a very confused woman. She was a Christian, her parents were professing Christians, and she was trying to live out what she saw as her biblical responsibility toward her parents. She sincerely wanted to practice the biblical admonition "Honor your father and your mother, that your days may be long upon the land which the LORD your God is giving you.[1] To her, honoring her father and mother meant being at their beck and call, anticipating their needs, and denying her own right to happiness.

As we talked together, I discovered that Sandra had a giving personality and was taken advantage of by almost everyone she met. Her boss at the travel agency where she worked would frequently assign her tasks that required unpaid overtime. Her two sons lived a life of leisure because Sandra waited on them hand and foot. She could never say no to her pastor or any other authority figure, so she was on every committee at the church. In fact, when she first came to see me, her question was not about how to deal with her demanding parents, but "Why am I so tired all the time?" The answer to that question wasn't hard to find: she was doing everything for everybody and getting no rest at all!

A PROBLEM IN TWO DIMENSIONS

I chose the story of Sandra as our starting point in this book—not because her story is unusual and sensational but rather because it is so commonplace. Sandra is typical of the kinds of people I see every day in my practice. She exemplifies the two dimensional nature of relationships: the dimension of the *past* and the dimension of the *present*. Some people who struggle in relationship to their parents have problems centered in the *past* dimension, others experience problems in the *present* dimension, and still others experience pain in *both* dimensions.

Those who are burdened with memories and emotions left over from physical abuse, sexual abuse, emotional abuse, neglect, or abandonment are dealing with the dimension of the past. Their parents may be nice people now. Or they may be dead or estranged and completely out of the picture. For whatever reason, the struggle these people have with their parents is about things that were said and done many years ago but which continue to hurt and hinder them in the present. It's hard for them to forgive and get over what has already happened.

I also meet a lot of people who struggle in the relationship they have with their parents right now. Even those who had a *Leave It To Beaver* childhood sometimes grow up to find that their parents have changed because of differences in their circumstances, their health, or their stage in life. They have become cranky, ill-tempered, self-centered, and demanding. Aging brings changes in our parents, and those changes can often be hard for us to accept and deal with.

Sandra, as it turned out, had struggles in both the past and present dimensions of her relationship with her parents. As I talked with her, I learned that her father—though a professing Christian and a church elder—had always been a hot-tempered and physically abusive man. If Sandra ever got out of line or said something her father didn't like, his response was to reach out and strike her, usually in the face or on the back of the head. More than once in her childhood, she had been hit until she was bruised and bleeding.

During one counseling session, as she talked about the abuse of the past, I asked her how old she was when this physical abuse ended. She looked at me as if I had just asked her a very strange question. Then she said, "It *never* ended."

It took me a moment to absorb what she was saying. Then I asked, "You mean, your father is in his sixties and you are in your forties, and he *still* hits you?"

She looked down at her hands, which she was wringing in her lap. "Yes," she said. "It happened again just the other day."

Here was a woman who had a less-than-ideal relationship (to put it mildly) with her parents in the past and who continues to experience pain, pressure, and manipulation from her parents today. And, being a conscientious Christian, her question to me is "How do I honor my father and my mother, like the Bible says? I feel guilty saying this, but the truth is I don't like them, I don't want to be around them—but I want to do the right thing. I want to honor them, but I don't know what *honor* means. How do I honor my father and mother when all they do is *dishonor* me?"

WHAT HONOR IS—AND ISN'T

From our earliest years, our parents have been virtual god-figures in our lives, wielding enormous power over our feelings and our sense of security and well-being. Even in adulthood, these two people loom large in our emotions and our subconscious minds. The thought of having a parent withdraw love and approval from us can be truly terrifying, even for adults. That is one reason why problems in our relationships with parents can be very stubborn and difficult to remedy. These issues have to be resolved on three different levels of our being: the *cognitive level* (what we think), the *behavioral level* (what we do), and the *emotional level* (how we feel).

The first and easiest level to reach is the cognitive level. In Sandra's case, one of the issues that was holding her back was her confused thinking about a Bible passage which said, "Honor your father and your mother." She didn't know, in a practical sense, what *honor* meant. Did it mean she had to forgive and forget the past? That she should ignore the past? Or should she try to *resolve* the past?

And what about the present? Did *honor* mean that she had

to submit to her father's verbal and physical abuse? That she had to accept her mother's manipulative hypochondria, coddling her every time she had a so-called "heart attack"? That she had to submit to her parents' unreasonable demands? What exactly is the responsibility of a forty-two-year-old adult to her parents?

Sandra and I spent a lot of time discussing what *honor* is—and isn't—from a biblical perspective. When the Bible says, "Honor your mother and father," the word *honor* means esteem, respect, and acknowledge. The original Hebrew word for honor means "to weight heavy," which conveys the image of an object (such as a piece of gold) that tips a balance scale heavily in one direction, indicating great value. In other words, to honor someone is to bestow value, worth, and significance upon that person. Honor cannot be extorted or demanded from us. True honor is a *gift* we give freely to another person.

Some people confuse *honor* with *obedience*, but there is a vast difference between these two concepts. *Obedience* suggests living under the command of another person and being subordinate to that person. An employee obeys the boss. An enlisted man obeys the commanding officer. A Christian obeys God. A minor child obeys his parents. When we obey, we submit to authority. There is a vertical relationship between the one who commands and the one who obeys.

But *honor* suggests maturity and mutuality in a relationship. We can honor a person without submitting ourselves to that person's command. We can honor our parents even after we reach the age of independence when we no longer must obey their authority. Honor is a completely separate concept from obedience. In a healthy family, children honor parents and parents honor children—but parents do not obey children. We honor each other when we affirm and respect the worth of each other.

Once we have clearly separated the concept of honor from the concept of obedience, we realize that honor does not mean giving in to unreasonable demands. Honor does not mean cooperating with a dysfunctional person in her unhealthy behavior. Honor does not mean excusing abusive behavior.

You can honor another person and still maintain boundaries between yourself and that person. You can honor another person and still limit that person's demands on your time. You can honor another person and still say, "I'm not going to talk to you on the phone every day. I'm not going to do things for you that you should do for yourself. I'm not going to allow you to abuse me any further. I'm not going to be your sole link to the outside world. Because I honor you, I want to help you to stop dishonoring yourself and to stop dishonoring me."

These are the concepts I began with in order to recalibrate Sandra's thinking. It was a relief for her to realize that *honor* did not have to mean being used, abused, and exploited. She found it fairly easy to grasp and absorb these truths on a cognitive level. But she found it much harder to make changes in the other two levels of her being: the behavioral level and the emotional level.

After each of our sessions together, Sandra went home determined to make positive changes in her behavior. She resolved not to let her parents manipulate her or make her feel guilty again. But before long, her parents would call and make some outrageous demand on her. At first, she would try to set firm limits. "No, Mom. No, Dad," she replied, "I can't do that." But then her mother would complain about chest pains or her Dad would start inflicting guilt or verbal abuse, and Sandra would fall right back into the old pattern.

INTERRUPTING THE CYCLE

There are cycles in every relationship, and when a relationship is unhealthy, one of the first items on the agenda is to break the cycle. In Sandra's case, the cycle went like this:

- Mom and Dad call and make a demand.
- Sandra responds by meeting that demand.
- The more Sandra responds, the more her mom and dad demand.
- Go back to the beginning and repeat.

My job as a therapist was to help Sandra interrupt that cycle. I said to her, "You have already changed your thinking on what it means to honor your father and mother. Now I want you to change your behavior to conform with your new thinking. When your parents make a demand, I want you to analyze that demand according to what you know you should and shouldn't do, and I want you to make a decision. If what they want is reasonable, you are free to agree to it. Don't just automatically say no and cut your parents off. But if what they ask of you is not reasonable or healthy, then say no. That's going to interrupt the cycle—and that's where you are going to have to stand firm.

"It may help to think of it as a chess game. When your parents make a demand, it is as if they are making a move on the chess board. You counter their move by saying no. Now, this cycle has been built up over the years and is very difficult to break. So the countermove on their part is to demand even louder and longer. You can expect them to pressure you with more guilt, more manipulation, more 'heart attacks,' more hitting—anything to restore the cycle and get you back into the role they want you to play. You need to be prepared for that countermove—and you need to brace yourself for the onslaught.

"Just understand that when you break the cycle, your parents' behavior is going to get worse, not better. They're going to tell you how ungrateful you are. They're going to quote 'Honor your father and your mother' to you. That's what you are going to have to withstand from your parents. It's going to be hard for you to stick to your guns and make those changes at the behavioral level.

"But that's not all. You are also going to be attacked from the inside, at the emotional level. Something inside you is going to say, 'This is wrong. I'm being a bad daughter. I'm hurting my parents. I'm dishonoring them. I'm sinning.' That is the voice of years of conditioning and false guilt. Practice turning that voice off. Persist in the behavior that you *know* is right, even though it *feels* wrong, until those feelings can be relearned."

It took a long time for Sandra to stand up to her parents and hold her ground. She tried again and again to draw healthy boundaries between herself and her mother, and again and again she succumbed to the guilt and manipulation. Whenever she got sucked back into the old pattern, we strategized together so that she could be stronger and better prepared to survive the next battle. In time, she scored a few small victories, then larger and larger victories.

One of the concepts that was most helpful for Sandra was the realization that what she had always thought of as honoring—giving in to being used and abused by her parents—was actually *hindering* and *harming* her parents. Once Sandra realized that her so-called "honor" was simply enabling her parents to build more infantile, demanding, dependent personalities, she was able to draw clear boundaries and say no to her parents, knowing that this was best not only for herself but for them as well.

Sandra expressed this healthy new outlook one day in counseling when she told me, "It used to be that whenever Mom said, 'Oh, my heart!' or Dad said, 'You're ungrateful— you're killing your mother.' I would just get all twisted up with guilt. But now, whenever they talk that way, I picture a whiny child throwing a tantrum: 'You're unfair! If you don't do what I say, I'm gonna hold my breath and turn blue and die, and then you'll be sorry!' They're being just that ridiculous! Once I get that picture in my mind, they lose their power to control me."

Today, Sandra has a much healthier relationship with her

parents. They still try to get their way, and Sandra still occasionally gives in when she shouldn't—but never as often as or to the same extent that she used to. She has told her father in no uncertain terms that he is never to raise a hand to her again, and he hasn't. Where there used to be hurt and confusion, there are now clear boundaries. For the first time in her life, Sandra feels like a full-fledged adult.

"My parents are not bad people," Sandra says today. "But they allowed their lives to revolve entirely around me, and that just wasn't healthy. It was hard for me to come to the realization that my own parents had some growing up to do. Our roles had become confused. They still treated me like a child, yet they also acted like children, making selfish demands on me. Now that some of the debris has been swept out of our relationship, I can appreciate their good qualities. Our roles are clearer now, and the most amazing thing has happened: I'm actually learning to *like* my parents!"

At every level of her life—the cognitive, the behavioral, and the emotional—Sandra has learned what it really means to "honor your father and your mother."

HOPE FOR YOU—AND THE PEOPLE WHO RAISED YOU

Sandra's situation—the problem of parents who make capricious and unreasonable demands—is one of the most common problems I see in my counseling practice. But I also see many people with equally common, equally troubling problems involving adult children and their parents:

- People who struggle with in-laws
- People whose aging parents are undergoing changes in health or personality, becoming an emotional burden or a financial burden or a time burden on their lives

- People who say, "My parents are divorcing and they want me to take sides"
- People whose parents overprotect and overcontrol
- People whose parents interfere with their child-rearing decisions
- People whose parents don't know how to love
- People whose parents are weak and unavailable
- People whose parents prophesied failure
- People whose parents have died, leaving a legacy of shame, pain, and bitterness behind

Perhaps you see your relationship with your own parents in one or more of those descriptions. Perhaps you can identify with Jonathan, a client of mine whose father never affirmed him when he was a child, never went to his basketball games, never thought he was good enough, never said "I love you." Jonathan left home at age sixteen, and he's had almost no contact with his father since. Now in his early thirties, Jonathan recently learned that his father is dying of cancer and hasn't long to live. So now Jonathan wants to know, "Should I try to reconcile with this distant, unfeeling stranger who has ignored me all these years—just because he happens to be my father, just because he's dying? Do I have to honor a father who has never honored me?"

Or perhaps you can identify with Amy. She was raised in a dysfunctional but nominally Christian family. Because her father is an alcoholic, she started attending a Twelve Step program for codependents. Thanks to the insight she gained in the program, she realized she had been enabling and rescuing her father—making excuses for him, cleaning up his messes, shielding him from the consequences of his addiction—when she should have been confronting his behavior with "tough love." Finally, she said to her father, "I'm not doing this anymore! You're not sick, you're drunk! Until you get sober, you're on your own!" When she stepped out of the enabler role, her entire family pressured her to return to the old pattern. Her sister pleaded with her, her dad swore at her, and her mother read Bible verses to her—all of them trying to get her to return to her former role. So Amy asked me, "Am I wrong to confront my dad's addiction? Can I honor my father and my mother while refusing to play along with their addiction and denial?"

Or perhaps you know how Kevin feels. His mother means well, but she tries to control his life. Kevin senses that God is calling him to the ministry, but his mother wants him to go to law school so that he can be successful and make a lot of money. When Kevin sat across the kitchen table from his mother and tried to explain his decision to become a pastor, she became sulky and quiet, refusing to even discuss the matter with him. So Kevin wants to know, "How can I follow my own conscience and be my own person and still honor my mother like the Bible says?"

Though I have changed names and other details in the stories I tell in this book and though some of these stories are composites of two or more situations, the people in these stories are real people and their problems are real problems. I'm sure you will identify with many of the issues and dynamics I describe in these pages.

The good news is that I have seen a lot of these people grow stronger and wiser in relating to their parents. I have seen their relationships with their parents improve. I have seen people who were controlled by others take control of their own lives. I have seen intergenerational cycles broken, so that people who received poor parenting learned how *not* to pass their hurt on to their own children. I have seen people plagued by guilt and tortured memories become liberated and satisfied.

And it can happen to you too.

These are tough times for parent/adult-child relationships. Parents are living longer. Health and economic fears are growing. Families are disintegrating. Mobility is separating generation from generation. These factors are taking a toll on our society, but they don't have to destroy the ties between you and your parents. If you have a good relationship with your parents, you can learn to make it better. If you have a strained relationship, you can learn to heal it. If you have a broken relationship, you can learn to restore it. If you have an absolutely intolerable relationship with your parents, you can learn to make it bearable.

My goal in this book is to apply Scripture and sound psychological principles to the increasingly complex problems that all adult children face as they relate to their parents. In the coming chapters, we will explore:

- The stages of parent/adult-child relationship: how to respond to each new phase of the journey
- How to set boundaries in your relationship with your parents—emotional boundaries, time boundaries, control boundaries, and financial boundaries
- How to deal with in-laws
- How to deal with the special problems of aging parents
- How to forgive your parents for what they did to you in the past and what they continue to do to you now
- How to break a destructive generational cycle so that your children can build healthy lives

We have just set out on a journey together—a journey of discovery and healing. The destination: a restored relationship with your parents, or, if that is not possible, at least a healing of your soul, your emotions, and your memories. In the next eleven chapters, you and I will uncover and explore the biblical truths, psychological insights, and practical strategies that will enable you to love, forgive, tolerate, and make peace with the people who raised you.

2

Why the Family?

Linda's father found her in the den, watching *The Three Stooges* on the old black-and-white TV. Linda loved the summertime, when she could spend hours playing with her Barbie dolls, drawing pictures of horses, and watching TV. "Linda," said her father, snapping off the TV as he entered the room, "come with me. I want to talk to you." Linda hated it when he did that—turning off the TV right in the middle of her shows—as if, at ten years old, she was not entitled to any consideration at all. Still, she knew better than to protest anything her father did.

Linda got up and followed her father down the hall, wondering what he wanted but afraid to ask. It wasn't unusual for her father to be home in the middle of the day. He never held any job longer than a few months at a time, and this was one of his between-jobs periods. Linda's mother was away, working at the cafeteria.

Her father stopped at his bedroom door and opened it. "In here," he said. Linda instantly felt a terrible sense of foreboding, but she went inside. Her thirteen-year-old brother, Pete, was already in the room, standing beside their parents' bed. He was looking away, his eyes not meeting Linda's.

Linda's father closed the door behind her, and suddenly she felt very trapped, very scared. She was too scared to ask the question that was uppermost in her mind: "What is all this about?"

Her father took a dollar bill off his bureau and stuffed it into one of the pockets on the skirt of Linda's dress. "Here's a dollar," he said. "I want you to do something for me. Now, there's nothing wrong with what I want you to do, but some people wouldn't understand. For example, your mother wouldn't understand. So you have to promise you'll never tell anyone."

"What do you want me to do?" Linda's voice was shaking. Her whole body trembled even though she didn't feel cold.

"I'm teaching your brother about the facts of life," he said. "And you're going to help me show your brother some things that boys need to know about."

It was more than thirty years after that day that Linda sat in my office and told me how her father used her to "teach" her brother about sex. That was just the first time her father and brother had sex with her. There were many others. And the questions Linda asked me, with pleading in her eyes, were: "What is a family for? My family destroyed my life. I've never been married and I never will be. I've tried, and I can't change the way I feel about myself or about men. I can't pray. I can't trust other people. My father's been dead for ten years, and I still curse his name every day of my life. Why did I have to be born into that family? Why couldn't I have been born into another family? Or why couldn't I have just been born dead?"

Why, indeed?

You see it on television talk shows, you hear it in the stories people tell in their support groups and recovery groups, and perhaps you have even felt the pain of it in your own child-hood and adolescence. For many people, the family is a literal hell on earth. It is the place where they have been abused and exploited; the place where they learned to hate themselves and see themselves as worthless; the place where their emotions were scarred, their memories were poisoned, and their personalities were distorted.

But does a family *have* to be that way? If so many families are so overwhelmingly destructive, then what good are families anyway? Wouldn't all of us be better off raised in state-run orphanages than being raised by these monsters called parents? I know many people who think so.

But while there are few things in this world as tragic and destructive as a disordered family, there are also few things more beautiful in this world than a family that functions as God intended it to.

THE FAMILY PLAN

The Bible is a family book. It presents the family as the basis of human society and the place where our emotional and relational well-being is to be formed. The Bible describes God as a Father, and it is through the example of godly parents that children are intended to form an understanding of the true nature of their Heavenly Parent, God.

The family is where we acquire our identity, our sense of who we are, where we come from, where we belong, what values we hold to. In the family, we are not merely individuals rattling around loose within four walls. We are members of a miniature society. It is in the family that we learn how to interact in a network of relationships. We learn how to get along with people. We learn gender roles. We learn how to relate to people who have more power than we do and to those who have less power than we do. We learn what it means to be part of a community and how to respect the rights and welfare of other family members.

The family is the basic training ground for all our relationships and interactions in adulthood. It is the crucible in which our souls, our psyches, are formed. We are molded by our experiences in the family—both postitive and negative

experiences. Even in the worst and most painful family circumstances, we are gaining the character and resources that
will enable us to survive out in the world. In our families, we
are persons in the making.

God designed families to be the vehicles for the transmission of tradition and continuity from one generation to the
next. Notice the wording of Exodus 20:12: "Honor your father
and your mother, *that your days may be long upon the land
which the* LORD *your God is giving you.*" That is a command
linked to a promise, and the promise is not that you will live to
be ninety-seven if you're kind to Mom and Dad. The Hebrew culture to which that promise was given took a long-term view of
family. They saw themselves as a link in an unbroken chain
stretching centuries upward through the line of their ancestors
and down the centuries through the line of their unborn descendents. God was saying to these people, in effect, "If you
honor your father and mother, and respect the traditions and values they have conveyed to you, then you will be laying a stable,
solid foundation for your descendents so that long after you are
gone, they will flourish in this land which I have given you."

Family tradition is very important. People need to experience
generational continuity. That is why God places this command
in the Bible.

The family, as God intended it to be, is a group of people
bound together in an understanding, a promise, a covenant of
caring for one another. Those parents who are faithful to their
calling to care for their children will teach their children to
trust. A healthy family functions this way:

- Individual family members are allowed to think their
  own thoughts and feel their own feelings. Their
  individuality is recognized and celebrated.
- Individual family members affirm and support one
  another.
- Communication is clear and free of distortions.
  Honesty creates an atmosphere of trust.

- There is a clear hierarchy. Mother and Father put each other first and support each other in directing the family.
- Family rules are flexible, discussable, and open for change.
- Family members have a healthy involvement with persons outside the family.
- The family has the ability to solve problems and negotiate the transitions that come with changes and with progression in the life cycle of the family.
- Family members can disagree with one another without destroying the bonds of the relationship.
- The family honestly faces and admits its problems and is willing to seek help when coping with those problems is beyond its resources.

Sounds wonderful, doesn't it? Unfortunately, not all of us grew up in families that meet this description.

SPOKEN AND UNSPOKEN RULES

Dean is thirty-eight years old, single, and living at home with Mom and Dad. He's bright and highly educated. In fact, he spent nine years in college, hopping from major to major, finally graduating (reluctantly, it seems) with a B.S. in Sociology. Although Dean has spent more than enough time in school to be a doctor or a lawyer, he has a part-time job at a supermarket stacking cans on shelves and asking, "Paper or plastic?" He doesn't date; in fact, he has no social life at all. He spends most of his time around the house watching TV.

Dean is a classic case of the overly-loved child. He is an only child, born to an older couple. (Mom was thirty-eight when he was born, Dad was forty; they are both now in their late seventies.) Dean's mother in particular has always coddled him, excused his mistakes, and never let him fail at anything. In fact, his parents have rarely let him *try* anything. He is very comfortable living at home, rent-free. It's the house he's lived in most of his life, so why should he leave? What's more, where would he go? He doesn't know how to take care of himself, he's never held a full-time job, he's never made any real, durable friendships out in the world. The fact is, *this* is his world—Mom and Dad and the house he grew up in.

What is wrong with this picture? Dean and his parents are too close, emotionally. They are what psychologists call *enmeshed*. Dean is an extension of his parents, and they are an extension of him—one cozy little family system. Though he's pushing forty, Dean is still Mommy and Daddy's darling baby boy. Dean has not negotiated the normal transitions of adulthood. In fact, both Dean and his parents have managed to avoid growing up. Mom and Dad have not had to release their son and face an empty nest, and Dean has not had to face the world as a man. Both parents and child operate on a set of unspoken rules which reinforce one another's dysfunction.

What are the *rules* in your family? I don't mean rules like "Feet off the coffee table," or "Don't leave the toilet seat up." I mean the rules—some spoken but most unspoken and unacknowledged—that govern how everyone in the family is supposed to act. Most of the rules in a family are hidden rules. They are very real and powerful, but they are seldom, if ever, taken out and examined. Many of these rules operate in the unconscious realm, and the members of the family are completely unaware of them until they are exposed with the help of a professional counselor.

The rules which governed Dean's family were rules such as "Nobody is allowed to change. Everything and everyone must stay exactly as they are," and "Nobody is ever to challenge Dean or make him feel uncomfortable in any way," and "Nobody is to form attachments or interests outside this family."

The enmeshed situation for Dean and his parents, in which each member of the family sees the rest of the family as an extension of himself, is a difficult problem to deal with. The members of the enmeshed system have erected massive emotional barriers of denial around their cozy little castle, and it is very difficult for anyone, even a professional counselor, to penetrate those barriers.

But the opposite of enmeshment—disengagement—can be an equally destructive and stubborn problem. In a disengaged family, all the members wrap themselves in their own individual worlds. They maintain tight boundaries around themselves, their thoughts, their feelings, their issues. There is little or no intimacy, self-disclosure, or vulnerability in the disengaged system. Family rules, though hidden, tend to be strictly defined, unbending, and inviolable: "You don't bother me, and I won't bother you. Don't talk to me about feelings. Stay out of my space. Leave me alone. This is my life. Mind your own business."

And there are many other rules, both spoken and unspoken, which govern (and often damage or destroy) our families. There are rules governing family communication. There are rules governing family secrets. And there are rules governing family coalitions. Let's look at each of these sets of rules in turn.

RULES ABOUT FAMILY COMMUNICATION

I once counseled an entire family—a father in his sixties, a son in his early forties, and two daughters in their thirties. Mom had died a few years earlier. The problem: Mom had always been the family switchboard. All family communication passed through her. If one sibling wanted to know about another sibling, she asked Mom. If a child wanted to approach Dad on some subject, he asked Mom to make the approach. If Dad needed to deal with one of his children about some issue, he had Mom convey the message.

When Mom died, no one in the family knew how to talk to anyone else in the family. There were no patterns, no skills, no "phone lines" in place for one member of the family to communicate clearly and directly to another. In this particular case, the problem was not terribly difficult to resolve. In fact, with only a few counseling sessions, we were able to uncover the problem and find ways of clearing up expectations and opening direct lines of communication.

This communication dynamic is called *triangling*. If there is a problem or issue between two people, they find themselves unable to come together and resolve it directly. One or both of them must pull a third person into the fray. A common form of triangling is when the parents fight (either overtly or covertly) and bring the child into the picture—either as a pawn or as a participant in the fight. Triangling happens in a very obvious way when two parents divorce and force the child to take sides.

But triangling can also take very subtle forms. One parent may attempt to influence or impress the child, hoping the child will carry a message to the other spouse. For example, Dad may mope around and act miserable in the presence of the child, hoping the child will go to Mom and say, "How can you treat Dad that way? Can't you see how unhappy you're making him?" Dad hasn't said a word, but he is triangling and manipulating like crazy.

Another common communication problem between parents and adult children is *double messages* or *incongruent messages*—communication in which two completely opposite messages are conveyed at the same time. A verbal double message occurs when one half of a sentence cancels out the other half: "I want you to be self-reliant," says Dad, "so do as I say." How do you respond to that? Do you become self-reliant and refuse to obey Dad, or do you do as Dad says?

And there is the double message in which the verbal and nonverbal messages cancel each other out: Mom tells you, "I forgive you," yet the stern tone of her voice, the glare in her eyes, and the way she stands with her fists pressed against her hips tell you she doesn't forgive you at all. When verbal and nonverbal messages conflict, it is almost always the nonverbal message that is true, not the words that come with it.

Parents who send double messages usually don't do so to be mean or difficult. They may be conveying mixed messages because they actually feel mixed emotions. We are all, in a sense, multiple personalities, capable of experiencing many conflicting thoughts and feelings at the same time. When Dad says, "I want you to be self-reliant, so do as I say," he is probably quite sincere. He does want you to be self-reliant—and he wants it so much that another part of him is willing to steamroll your self-reliance and force you to be self-reliant on his terms! And when Mom says, "I forgive you," she probably believes she really has forgiven you. Meanwhile, another part of her simply refuses to acknowledge the anger that continues to seethe within her at an unconscious level.

All of us have engaged in double messages from time to time. Some people, however, resort to double messages on such a constant basis that it creates a seriously distorted and unhealthy communication pattern. This can be a very frustrating issue to deal with. A pathological double-message communicator is difficult to pin down and difficult to have a meaningful conversation with, especially in times of conflict: "Why, I never meant any such thing! My dear, you seem to be the one with the problem. You're always reading hidden meanings into what I say!"

In a healthy family, communication is clear, direct, and free of distortions. Healthy family relationships are marked by honesty and trust. Triangling and continual double messages are signs that something isn't working right in the family communication system.

RULES ABOUT FAMILY SECRETS

Linda, the woman at the beginning of this chapter who was sexually abused by her father and brother, once went to her mother to tell her about the abuse. By that time, Linda was an adult in her mid-thirties, and her father had been dead for five years. Linda felt sure that her mother knew about the incest and did nothing to stop it.

Linda and her mother were in the living room of her mother's home. "Mom," said Linda, "I want to talk to you about Daddy."

"Oh?"

"I want to tell you something I should have told you a long time ago."

"Oh." Her mother looked at her with a face that was frozen and expressionless.

"When I was little, from the time I was ten until I was about fifteen, Daddy sexually abused me. And he also let Pete do it to me."

Linda's mother didn't move, didn't speak. Her eyes, which had been looking into Linda's, now seemed to stare right through her as if she wasn't there. For several long seconds it was as if she was in suspended animation, as if time had stopped.

Suddenly her mother looked away. "Oh, goodness! Look at the time!" she said, rising to her feet and hurrying to the television set. "*The Price is Right* is on. I never miss that show. I just think that Bob Barker is so debonair, don't you?" She clicked the set on and started flipping channels.

"Mom, I wanted to talk—"

"Oh, we can talk during the show, dear. During the commercials."

"Mom, didn't you hear what I told you? About Daddy?"

"Why don't you go out and make some popcorn, dear, and we'll watch the show together."

Linda never brought the subject up again.

What happened here? Linda had broken the rules about her family's dirty little secrets. The rules of Linda's family were "We never talk about what Daddy did," and "If anyone does talk about what Daddy did, then we ignore it and make it go away."

Many families have such secrets. They may not be as dark

and shameful as incest, but there are "things we just don't talk about." Certain issues are kept from certain family members. We don't talk about Sally's breast cancer or Dad's alcoholism or Mom's spendaholism or why Tommy was out all night. The secret nature of these issues actually intensifies their emotional impact. Those who know the secret often align themselves against those who don't, creating tension and conflict—and some of the people involved haven't a clue as to what it's all about!

In a healthy family, secrets are brought out into the light and honestly examined so that their destructive power can be defused. Family secrets—issues which are off-limits and forbidden and denied—are a sign that something isn't working right in the family communication system.

RULES ABOUT FAMILY COALITIONS

The Bible is full of examples of the same family dynamics I deal with in my counseling practice every day. Clearly, disordered families have been around as long as there have been families. While the Bible contains the blueprint for a healthy family, it also contains many negative examples which serve as case studies that we can examine and learn from. One such example is the story of a father named Isaac, his wife Rebekah, and his sons Jacob and Esau. The story is found in Genesis 27.

Old, blind, and bedridden, Isaac knew his time on earth was short, so he called his older son Esau to his side and asked him to kill and prepare some wild game for him. When Esau had brought Isaac this meal, Isaac would give him his final blessing.

But Rebekah was listening at the door of the tent and heard what was said between Isaac and Esau. So she ran to Jacob, the younger son, and hatched a plan whereby Jacob would trick Isaac into giving him the blessing intended for Esau. What we see in this story is a classic case of *coalitions* within a family. Isaac and his favorite son Esau are teamed up in opposition to Rebekah and her favorite son Jacob. The basic structure of the family has been ripped apart.

Healthy families are families in which there is a clear hierarchy. Mom and Dad put each other first and support each other in caring for the children. Healthy families resolve conflict and issues openly and honestly in an atmosphere of trust.

HONORING DISHONORABLE PARENTS

At this point, we have looked at what a healthy family is supposed to look like—how it was designed and intended by God to function as a nurturing, protective environment for the development of a child's personality. We have also recognized that not all families are created equal. Families often take some very unhealthy forms. Perhaps you recognize some of the dynamics of your own family in these descriptions of families which are enmeshed, disengaged, triangling, secretive, or divided into coalitions.

How can you respond in a healthy way to these unhealthy situations? How should you go about honoring parents who have consistently dishonored you? These are some of the questions we will explore in detail in the next few chapters. We will start with a framework of presuppositions:

First, you may have had a painful childhood, but that was not your responsibility. You are responsible for building a healthy life right now. There are connections between your childhood and your adult life, but those connections don't have to run—or ruin—your life in the present.

Second, you are a separate person from your parents. You are entitled to think your own thoughts and feel your own feelings. You are an adult, and you are responsible for becoming your own person. Accepting that responsibility can be uncomfortable, but it is the key to overcoming the painful emotions, memories, and habits of the past.

Third, you are committed to looking honestly at your relationship with your parents. You are committed to uncovering and defusing the explosive secrets of the past. You refuse to let those secrets hurt you and control you any longer. You are committed to opening the lines of communication and reexamining the unspoken rules of your family. Wherever you find unhealthy rules (such as "We don't talk about that," or "We don't acknowledge feelings"), you are committed to changing those rules and replacing denial with truth. As Jesus said, "And you shall know the truth, and the truth shall make you free."[1]

Fourth, you are committed to confronting and dismantling any unhealthy control and power your parents may have held over your behavior or your feelings, whether they are living or dead. You can honor your parents even as you remove yourself from under their domination. You can honor your parents even as you confidently and fully assume the role of a self-reliant adult.

These are some of the principles that Linda has used to regain control over her life after being abused by one parent and ignored by the other. Linda never was able to confront her father with the pain and the shame that he had inflicted on her; he died before she developed the insight and the inner strength to talk to him about it. And Linda was never able to penetrate the wall of denial that her mother erected around herself.

But Linda is her own person. She is no longer imprisoned by the secrets of the past or the unspoken rules of her family. She has learned to accept what happened to her in her childhood, not because it was a good thing but because God brought His good out of even such a terrible thing as incest. Linda has learned to find strength and resiliency in the broken places of her life. There are still broken places in her memories and her feelings that are yet to be mended, but Linda is making progress. On the whole, she is a happy and positive person.

And you can be, too.

In chapter 3, we will take the next step of our journey together as we examine the various stages and transitions in our relationship with our parents.

3

Seasons of Life

"**M**other, this is Angie," Don said nervously. He stepped quickly from Angie's side to his mother's, leaving Angie standing alone, looking a little scared, as if she was being presented for inspection.

"Why, Donnie, she's a lovely girl!" said Don's mother. "Much prettier than the last girl you brought by." Then, winking at Angie, she added, "Donnie has so many girlfriends, you know."

"Mother! I do not!"

"What about that red-haired girl, what was her name? Alison? You're still going out with her, aren't you?"

"Mother, I haven't seen her since—"

"Oh, it's not important. They come and they go, who can keep track." She motioned to Angie. "Come into the living room, dear." She steered her son over to the divan and pulled him down next to herself, while indicating a stiff-backed chair across the room for Angie. "Sit down, dear. Sit, sit, sit."

Angie sat. Don noted a look in her eyes that he had seen before—the look of a trapped animal.

"You seem a little older than most of Donnie's girls," Don's mother continued, eyeing Angie appraisingly.

"She's twenty-two, Mother," said Donnie, "the same age as me."

"I only meant that she's mature, Donnie. I don't mean she's too old for you," said his mother. Then she turned back to Angie. "Donnie is a wonderful boy but a little too sensitive. He nitpicks everything I say. But I'm not complaining, mind you. He's a sweet boy. He's been such a comfort to me ever since his father died fourteen years ago. He takes such good care of me and sees to all of my needs. I don't know what I would do without him."

The conversation continued for another half hour. Don's mother did most of the talking. Finally, Angie stood and said, "It's been very nice meeting you, but I really must go."

"Before you go," said Don's mother, "you should have Donnie show you around the house. This is where all of our beautiful memories are stored, isn't it, Donnie? Why don't you show her your room, Donnie? You know, Angie, dear, Donnie sleeps in the very same room he's had since he was three years old. I think it's wonderful that a boy can have such a secure and stable life, don't you?"

Finally, Don and Angie emerged from the house and got in Don's car. "I think Mother really liked you, Angie," Don said hopefully as he backed the car out of the driveway.

"Yeah." Angie sat with her arms folded, her eyes distant. "Could you take me home, Donnie—I mean, Don. I—I think I'm getting a headache."

Don pulled the car out onto the street. "Angie," he said, "I've got tickets to the concert tomorrow night. Shall I pick you up at seven?"

"I don't think so, Don. I'm going to be busy tomorrow night."

"Oh. Okay. Well, then how about Saturday? We could—"

"Look, Don, I'll call you, okay? Let's not make any plans just yet."

Don sighed. He had heard all of this before. His mother had won again. She had scared off another girlfriend.

Don's situation is an extreme form of a problem I see very often: an adult child fails to make the transition into adulthood. There is a very common dynamic at work in Don's problem. A single parent clings to the child for emotional support, refusing to let the child grow up, leave home, and assume a fully adult role in the world. Often (though not always), this dynamic takes place between a parent and a child of the opposite sex, so that this arrangement has the appearance of a pseudo-marriage. Whenever any outsider (such as a girlfriend or boyfriend) comes into the picture, the parent attacks. It may be an overtly hostile attack, or it may be subtle and manipulative, as in Don's case.

The normal pattern is for children to gradually form identities separate from their parents, beginning in infancy and continuing through their teen years. Then, as they emerge from their teens into their twenties, they court, marry, and move away. Sometimes, as in Don's case, this pattern can be disrupted or derailed. That is one of the problems that can arise in the early stages of the parent/adult-child relationship.

Our relationship with our parents takes on different hues at different times of life. In this chapter we will examine how our roles and relationships change as we and our parents grow older together.

STAGE 1: WE STEP INTO ADULTHOOD

In our late teens and early twenties, we are grasping for independence while still relying on our parents for some of our needs. Our task in this stage is to learn responsibility. We are finding out what it means to accept the consequences for our actions, thoughts, and feelings. In this stage, the focus in the adult child's relationship with Mom and Dad shifts from *obedience* to *honor*. This shift is symbolized in the traditional marriage ceremony: the father of the bride escorts his daughter down the aisle, where he is asked, "Who gives this woman to be wed?" He replies, "Her mother and I." There is a clear dividing line at this point in the ceremony—and in the parent-child relationship. No longer is this woman a child under the authority of her parents. Her allegiance has shifted from her family of origin to the new family she is forming in partnership with her husband.

It is not uncommon, however, for parents to miss the point of this part of the ceremony. Often, even after a marriage has taken place, the parents of either the bride or the groom continue to demand primary allegiance from their married child. This is an unhealthy and unfair demand. As Genesis 2:24 tells us, "Therefore a man shall leave his father and mother and be joined to his wife, and they shall become one flesh." Or, to use the terminology of the original King James Version, they *leave* their parents, they *cleave* to each other, they *become* one.

You cannot cleave to your parents at the same time you cleave to your spouse. Yet many young adults find it difficult to leave their parents, even after they are married. They may *physically* move out of their parents' house and get a house or apartment of their own, but *emotionally* and *relationally* they are still part of the old family unit.

Why is leaving so difficult for some adult children?

In some cases, the problem lies within the adult child. He has never developed the confidence and sense of responsibility to care for himself. So this person remains dependent upon his parents, both emotionally and financially.

In other cases, the parents have created a series of roadblocks in the child's path, in order to delay the letting go process and avoid facing an empty nest. An example of this situation is the case of Don's mother, who chases off his girlfriends so that she can keep her "Donnie" all to herself.

June's husband is a sales executive for a food distributor. His territory encompasses most of the southeastern United States, so he is on the road six months out of the year. Consequently, June is very lonely, and has drawn close to her twenty-year-old daughter Celia for friendship and support. June loves to tell everyone what great buddies she and Celia are—how they play tennis together, shop together, go to movies together, and generally have a great old time together. The problem is that Celia doesn't want to be her mother's "buddy." She wants a life of her own, but whenever she tries to get out of doing something with June so she can go on a date or just do something by herself for an hour or two, June acts hurt and resentful. So Celia comes to my office and asks, "How can I have some space and some boundaries in my relationship with my mother?"

Jeff is twenty-five years old and lives at home. He is out of college and has a good job with a cellular phone company. His parents have had a troubled marriage for years. Whenever Mom and Dad deal directly with each other, they fight, and the fights can be quite ugly. So, in order to avoid that ugliness, the family has fallen into a pattern whereby Mom and Dad communicate through Jeff. Jeff has become the translator, the mediator, the diplomatic channel for all their communication, and thus peace (of a sort) is preserved in the family. Now Jeff is afraid to leave home. "I can't move out!" he tells me. "If I leave, they'll either get a divorce or they'll kill each other. I couldn't bear to have that on my conscience."

The problem facing these adult children is enmeshment. They are not allowed to be independent individuals with their own goals, thoughts, and outside relationships. The boundaries between these adult children and their parents is blurred. An enmeshed person is a person whose selfhood is being smothered and who is viewed by the rest of the family *not* as an individual but as an extension of themselves.

In her book *Toxic Parents*, Dr. Susan Forward provides a checklist of beliefs and says that if you hold four or more of these beliefs, then you are still very much enmeshed with your parents. Those beliefs (which I have slightly adapted) are:

_____ **It is up to me to make my parents happy.**
_____ **It is up to me to make my parents proud.**
_____ **I am my parents' whole life.**

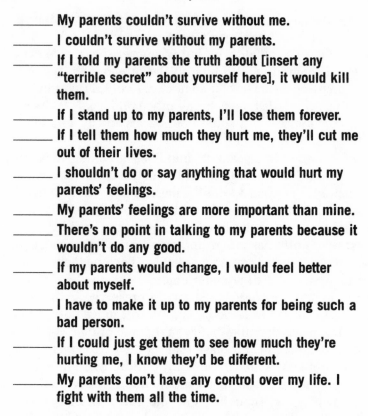

_____ My parents couldn't survive without me.

_____ I couldn't survive without my parents.

_____ If I told my parents the truth about [insert any "terrible secret" about yourself here], it would kill them.

_____ If I stand up to my parents, I'll lose them forever.

_____ If I tell them how much they hurt me, they'll cut me out of their lives.

_____ I shouldn't do or say anything that would hurt my parents' feelings.

_____ My parents' feelings are more important than mine.

_____ There's no point in talking to my parents because it wouldn't do any good.

_____ If my parents would change, I would feel better about myself.

_____ I have to make it up to my parents for being such a bad person.

_____ If I could just get them to see how much they're hurting me, I know they'd be different.

_____ My parents don't have any control over my life. I fight with them all the time.

By the way, it may surprise you that the last belief in that list is an indicator of enmeshment, but it's true. Being locked in combat with your parents can be as much a form of enmeshment as being a meek and submissive appendage to the family. Rebellion against parents is a normal part of adolescence, but it is not a healthy condition for people in their twenties, thirties, and beyond. The person who is enmeshed in conflict with her parents is incapable of making independent, proactive choices because she is too busy reacting against the wishes of Mom and Dad.

Rob was enmeshed in conflict with his parents. In his late twenties, he lived his entire life as an act of rebellion against

Mom and Dad. He had been planning a vacation in Yosemite, but then his mother suggested he take some time off and go to Yosemite! To prove he was his own person, he told her, "I'm not taking any time off! And if I did, Yosemite would be the *last* place I'd go!" Later, Rob bought a slightly used Porsche 911 Cabriolet—it cost him half a year's salary—and showed it to his dad. He had his arguments all lined up for Dad's inevitable lecture on wasteful spending, but Dad loved the car and said, "I think you deserve it, son." Rob sold the car the next day. But Rob really knew he had a problem when he began to reconsider his marriage plans because his parents *approved* of his fiancée! As Dr. Paul Ware, psychoanalyst and neurologist at Louisiana State University, has said, "You know you have emerged from adolescence and become a full-fledged adult when you do what *you* want to do, even if your parents want you to as well."

If you find that you are in an enmeshed relationship with your parents, then it's time to start reprogramming your thinking. If you do not have the ability to change your belief system by yourself—and few people do—then I would encourage you to see a counselor who can help you find a healthy and balanced relationship with your parents.

A healthy, independent, adult relationship with your parents begins with these truths:

You are not responsible for your parents' feelings. You can't *cause* your parents to feel happy or sad or angry. Yes, your actions can affect others, but you are not responsible for the way other people feel, including your parents.

Being a "good son" or a "good daughter" does not mean you must always agree with or obey your parents. Sometimes the most loving thing you can do for your parents is to tell them a painful truth. If you do so, they may feel hurt or angry at first, but that doesn't mean it was wrong to tell them the truth. That only means that, like iodine on a wound, the truths that heal sometimes sting for a little while.

You can change, even if your parents choose not to. You can grow, even if your parents choose not to. You can become healthy and feel good about yourself, even if your parents try to hold back your growth and manipulate your feelings. You are your own person.

In counseling enmeshed people such as Don, Celia, and Jeff, I have encouraged them to look at their relationships in terms of their responsibility as an adult child. I ask, "What is your true responsibility to your parents? Is it to coddle them along, humor them, patronize them, make sure they never feel upset or uncomfortable? Or is it your responsibility to seek the highest, truest good for your parents—their emotional and relational health? Is being this close a positive thing in your parent's life? Does it block them from getting on with their lives? How long do you plan to tolerate the pain of this unhealthy relationship? Another year? Two years? Ten years? As long as your parents are alive?"

Don, Celia, and Jeff realized that they were doing their parents no favor by remaining in an enmeshed relationship with them. They proceeded to draw healthy boundaries in those relationships. In each case, they had to sit down with their parents and have a very difficult and honest talk. They had to endure their parents' strong emotions—including grief, hurt, and anger. They had to move away from their parents' homes. And then they had to continue communicating with their parents in an effort to heal the hurt caused when they "surgically removed" themselves from their enmeshed relationships. There is a price to pay for moving, growing, and changing. But each of these people paid that price—and they all agreed it was a bargain.

STAGE 2: WE BECOME EQUALS AS INDEPENDENT ADULTS

Liz is thirty-two, single, a mid-level manager with a large California-based financial institution, and a sincere Christian. She came to me several years ago, struggling with an intense weight of guilt and low self-esteem. "For the past two years," she said, "I've been having an affair with a married man, a man in my office. I initiated the affair. In fact, I pursued him even after he repeatedly rejected my advances. I'm just no good."

As we delved into her situation, I learned that after each of her trysts with this man, she could hear an accusing voice in her head: "You can't be trusted, Liz. You're just no good."

"Whose voice do you hear?" I asked.

"My mother's. That's exactly what she used to say to me all the time when I was growing up."

"Why did she say that to you?"

"I don't know."

"What kinds of things did you do that made your mother feel you couldn't be trusted?"

"I can't think of anything."

"Did you lie?"

"All kids lie once in a while."

"Did you lie very often?"

"Hardly ever. I've always been terrible at lying. My face always gave me away. I was painfully honest as a child."

"Did you steal things? Did you cheat? Why did your mother say you couldn't be trusted?"

"I don't know. I tried to be a model child, but I remember always feeling I was being misjudged. So I'd try harder, and still my mother didn't trust me. 'You can't be trusted, Liz,' she'd say. 'You're just no good.'"

"Does your mother still say such things to you?"

Liz seemed startled by the question. Something clicked. "You know, she does. I didn't realize until just now, but she still tells me I'm no good. She uses different words, but the message is the same. About the time I turned twenty-eight or twenty-nine, she started in on me: 'A nice girl should be married by the time she's your age.' And she kept asking whether I was using contraceptives and telling me there are a lot of men out there with AIDS. She had some crazy idea that if I was single and pursuing a career, then I must be living a wild promiscuous lifestyle. But I wasn't. I never did anything wrong—until I initiated this affair two years ago. But I guess she turned out to be right after all, didn't she?"

"Was she right, Liz? Or did she set up a prophecy for your life that, on some unconscious level, you felt duty-bound to fulfill? Could it be that after being told from childhood until now that you are 'just no good,' that you 'can't be trusted,' you believed it and went out in search of some way to make it true? I'm just asking the question. Only you can answer it."

And Liz did answer it in her own mind and emotions. It was true, and it was the missing piece of the puzzle of her behavior. She had known all along that she didn't really love the man she was involved with. What she hadn't understood was what motivated her be in a relationship that her conscience and religious beliefs told her was wrong and harmful.

Armed with the knowledge that she was acting out her mother's misguided prophecy, she quickly ended the affair. From then on, whenever her mother would make a judgmental comment about her, Liz firmly responded, "Mother, you have no reason to think such a thing of me. I'm not a terrible person. I'm a Christian, and I'm trying to live my life the way God wants me to. If you don't trust me, that's your problem, not mine. But I won't listen to you tear me down anymore." Liz's mother was stunned the first time Liz confronted her. It took only two or three more such confrontations for those judgmental comments to cease altogether. Liz had graduated to Stage 2.

In Stage 2 of the parent/adult-child relationship, we begin to enjoy a new plateau in the relationship with our parents. Once, the need for parental approval motivated much of our behavior. But at this point in life, the need for parental approval is no longer a valid motivation. Some of us may never obtain that approval, yet we must all learn to get on with our lives, with or without it.

Fred, a man in his forties, was the eldest of four siblings. Since childhood, he and his siblings had been engaged in competition for their father's approval, attention, and affection. This rivalry had become so ridiculous that Fred would sometimes get a call from one of his siblings, who would gloat, "I just got off the phone with Dad. We had a great, long talk. Gee, how long has it been since Dad called you? Months, isn't it?"

What triggered this rivalry in the first place? Fred's father had always withheld attention and affection from Fred and his siblings, dispensing his approval much like an animal trainer uses treats to get a dog to jump through hoops. Through counseling, however, Fred came to understand that a parent's affirmation should be offered unconditionally, not as a manipulative "treat." Having gained that insight, he took himself out of the competition for his father's attention. His dad's approval was no longer a prize he wanted to win. In fact, he finally realized that *real* unconditional acceptance and affirmation would always be out of reach anyway.

From then on, whenever his siblings tried to goad him with some crumb of attention their father had tossed their way, Fred would just say, "That's great. I'm glad you and Dad have such a good relationship." Fred had graduated to Stage 2. Like Fred, you *can* become your own person and assume your place as a full-fledged adult in this world, *whether or not you ever attain the approval of your parents.*

That doesn't mean we don't care about our parents' feelings. In fact, the key to resolving tension and conflict with a disapproving parent may lie in understanding *why* that parent behaves the way he does. And one of the most common reasons many parents use their approval as a tool for manipulation is *fear.* They are afraid of losing a piece of their identity, which they have invested in their children.

Most of us are aware that we have received much of our identity from our parents, but few of us stop to realize that, in a very real sense, our parents also derive a portion of their identity from us! That may be one of the reasons our parents have not yet learned to treat us as equals.

Richard is an attorney in his late twenties, the son of an attorney. Richard's father has a successful private practice in a small city and even served his community for four years as a deputy district attorney. Throughout his younger years, Richard's dad pushed him to get straight As and to set his sights on a distinguished career. "You've got the brains to be a great trial lawyer—another F. Lee Bailey," his father told him. "But you're not using your brains. You're not working as hard as you could. Son, if you would only apply yourself, start making the right moves and the right friends, why someday you could even be a senator or a Supreme Court justice. But keep going the way you're going, and you'll end up a junior partner in some little firm in West Overshoe."

Richard liked law, but he didn't like being pushed. No matter what Richard accomplished, no matter what honors he amassed (and they were considerable), he never could gain his father's approval. When Richard chose the "wrong" law school, his father was furious and refused to speak to him for months. And after graduation, when Richard chose the "wrong" area of specialization and joined the "wrong" law firm, he got into a loud argument with his father. It ended when Richard stormed out of his father's house and left two stripes of smoking Goodyear on his dad's driveway.

A few weeks later, Richard's mother called, begging him to reconcile with his father. She listened patiently as he fumed and raged about his father. "You know, Mom, " he concluded, "I don't even want to go into politics or sit on the Supreme Court! Those are Dad's goals, not mine! Why can't he just let me be a good lawyer with a good firm in nice little town? That was good enough for him! Why can't that be good enough for me?"

"That's just it," said his mother. "That wasn't good enough for him. When your father and I were first married, he told me all his dreams. He was ambitious, he really wanted to be *somebody*. Everything he says you can be—a senator, a Supreme Court justice, a world famous trial attorney—these were once *his* dreams. Time passed, and one day he realized that the most fame he would ever achieve was four years as a deputy district attorney. So he began to dream his dreams through you. That doesn't excuse anything he's done to you. I know he's wrong. He shouldn't try to live his life through you. But before you judge him too harshly, I hope you'll put yourself in his shoes and imagine what it feels like to watch a dream die."

Richard thought about what his mother told him. He had never realized before that his father saw himself as a failure. He had always viewed his father as a powerful, successful man. For the first time in his life, Richard saw his father not as a tower of authority and stubborn strength but as a rather sad middle-aged man who had fallen far short of his goals. Maybe Richard could never win his father's approval, but somehow that hardly seemed important anymore. He understood that the one who really needed approval and affirmation was his father. The moment he came to that realization, Richard had reached Stage 2 in his relationship to his dad.

A few months later, at a party for his parents' thirtieth wedding anniversary, Richard raised his glass and led a toast to his mother. Then he turned to his father, raised his glass again, and said, "And to a great man and a great father. Dad, you taught me to work hard and to be the best I can be. You've instilled a lot of yourself in me, and it's a privilege for me to carry that part of you with me into the future. Thank you, Dad." By the time they drank the toast, both Richard's and his father's eyes were glistening.

Richard demonstrated a lot of wisdom that day. He was able to assure his father that a part of his identity would be passed to the next generation, and in the process, Richard secured for himself a sense of wholeness and independence in his own identity. Our parents long to see a part of themselves reflected in us. When they are able to see that reflection, they often feel less need to control or manipulate our lives.

STAGE 3: WE TRADE ROLES
WITH OUR PARENTS

"When I was a kid," says Ted, "my dad was my best pal. He taught me how to tie my shoes. He told me stories about his war experiences. He taught me to love God and respect the flag and treat people fairly. I saw him cry only once when I was growing up, and that's when his brother, my Uncle Will, died of cancer. My dad was the strongest guy I knew. No one knew as much about fixing cars as he did. My dad never made much money, but he always took care of his family. It seemed like the world would always keep turning around as long as my dad was on it.

"But three years ago, my dad had a stroke. He couldn't talk anymore. He could hardly do anything for himself anymore. The past few months, my dad has had to wear diapers. I changed a lot of those diapers myself. And I had to watch this big, strong man who molded my life and my values, who taught me everything really important in life; I had to watch him sit with his head in his hands, bawling like a baby. And it tore my heart out. I know I'll miss him terribly when he's finally gone, but for his sake, I hope he goes soon."

According to *Newsweek* (August 16, 1990), the average American woman will spend seventeen years raising children . . . and *eighteen* years helping aging parents. More that six million elderly Americans need assistance to perform such basic tasks as getting out of bed and going to the bathroom. Millions more are unable to manage meal preparation, money, or transportation. For most of us, a time is coming when we will trade roles with our parents. The people we depended on in childhood will become our dependents.

This is often the hardest relationship stage for both parents and their adult children. For adult children like Dan and Susan, the question is, "Should Mom live with us? She certainly can't take care of herself, but we'd feel awful putting her in a nursing home. Yet we just don't have the room or the time or the finances to take care of her in our home. What should we do?"

For Helen, the question is, "What do I do about my brothers and sister? I have to drive forty miles round trip every day to visit Dad in the convalescent home. My siblings all live closer to Dad, yet they hardly ever visit him at all. If Dad needs anything, I'm the one who gets the call. The rest of my family doesn't lift a finger. I don't mind looking after Dad, but why do I have to shoulder the burden alone?"

For Mike, the question is, "How do I honor my mother, who has Alzheimer's? Her personality has completely changed. It's as if the sweet, loving person I knew is gone, and a mean, hostile thing has taken over her body. I can't stand watching her go through this. That disease has stolen her dignity and her humanity. Is this person still, in some real sense, my mother? Is she suffering? Is there some sense in which I, as a Christian, am expected to honor this shell that used to be my mother?"

These are all questions we will examine in greater detail in chapter 10. But as we take this first glance at Stage 3, the role reversal between ourselves and our parents, it is important that we try to see this stage of life from the our parents' perspective.

Faye, age eighty-nine, spends her days in a convalescent home. Her mind is strong even if her body is not. She remembers when she had so much to live for. Now, her days are meaningless and empty. "I'm just in the way," she says. "If I could just go and be with the Lord, my children would be better off. I hate to be such a burden on them. They have their own lives to lead, yet they feel they have to come visit me every weekend."

Raymond is in his seventies. He lives alone in an apartment and takes care of most of his own needs. His son would visit

Raymond more often, but Raymond's daughter-in-law is very demanding and has always disliked him. "I'm not senile, nor am I dependent," says Raymond, "but I do wish I could see my son and my grandkids more often. If my daughter-in-law doesn't want to come see me, well, that's okay. But why does she have to be so bossy? Why does she have to keep me out of my son's life and out of my grandkids' lives?"

Sherman and Elizabeth have built a comfortable retirement for themselves. They aren't rich, but they are able to maintain a condo and do a little traveling on the income from their investments and Social Security. But now their son has come to them asking for a financial bailout—to the tune of $50,000. "My son said to me, 'Dad, I know you've got the money, and you know I'll pay it back,'" says Sherman. "Well, I don't know anything of the sort! He says it's for a 'business opportunity,' but he won't give me any details about this so-called opportunity. He's always chasing one get-rich-quick scheme after another. We lent him ten thousand dollars just two years ago, and we never saw it again. Are we supposed to impoverish ourselves at our age so that he can grab some fly-by-night 'business opportunity'?"

The feelings and issues that aging people have to face include:

- *Impaired health.* The body begins to break down. Illnesses become more serious, chronic, and debilitating. The possibility of accidents becomes more acute due to decreased agility, eyesight, and hearing.
- *Increased isolation.* Older people often lack the means and the stamina to travel and visit friends and family. Many long-time friends have died or moved away. Loneliness, boredom, resignation, and a sense of uselessness are common features of aging.
- *Fear of death.* The aging person is acutely aware that most of her life is already past. Death

approaches. As frightening as death itself may be, even more frightening is the prospect of being abandoned by loved ones and having to face the final journey alone.

- *Infirmity or the fear of infirmity.* It is not uncommon for people to end their lives in a state of infirmity and helplessness: paralyzed by stroke, bereft of memory or mental acuity, unable to hear or see, or, most frightening of all, left in a vegetative state, dependent upon a respirator and feeding tubes. These prospects are an older person's worst nightmare.

Given the fears and issues facing an older person, it is not surprising that aging parents become almost childlike, looking to us for help and comfort. It can be a disconcerting experience to move into a Stage 3 role reversal with our parents. We are used to viewing them as the people we turn to for help and advice—not the other way around! How will we respond to our parents as they become more childlike and dependent upon us?

The experience can be exasperating. Some parents become demanding tyrants. They want you to do everything for them, and if you don't, they are quick to brand you as ungrateful. They don't hesitate to remind you how they gave the best years of their lives taking care of you. Others become martyrs. They suffer the indignities of old age bravely, and they make sure everyone around them knows it! Still others may become irrational. They develop strange fears or paranoias, and it becomes absolutely impossible to reason with them.

Added to this emotional frustration is the fact that caring for older parents places a burden on your time, finances, energy, and freedom. You may even experience bouts of wishing they were dead—followed by pangs of guilt and remorse. These are common feelings, and you should freely forgive yourself and accept God's forgiveness for these emotions.

WITHOUT REGRETS

Spring turns to summer. Then comes fall, and finally the cold of winter. These are the seasons of the year, and the seasons of a human life. We are children and adolescents in the spring. In the summer we leave our parents and step into adulthood. In the fall, we become equals with our parents and assume the role of fully independent adults. In the winter, we trade roles with our parents.

The seasons go 'round and 'round. The world keeps turning. For most of us, there is a feeling of foreverness about family. We gather with parents and grandparents, children and grandchildren, around a wedding altar, a backyard barbecue, a Thanksgiving turkey, or a Christmas tree. And sometimes, we gather around a grave, where we commemorate a life that has just been completed. If we approach each stage of the parent/adult-child relationship thoughtfully, with maturity and love and a desire to seek the best for everyone concerned, then we will be able to walk away from that graveside without regrets.

In the next chapter, we will look at the special hurdles and hindrances that face us if we were loved too little—or too much—by our parents.

4

Too Much Love or Too Little Love?

One night when Jason was in the fourth grade, he went to his mother in a panic and begged her to help him with his project in California history. He had to write a report and make a relief map of the state out of modeling clay. "When is all this due?" she asked.

"Tomorrow morning," he admitted.

"It's half an hour till bedtime and you tell me it's due tomorrow morning?" she exclaimed. "When was it assigned?"

"Five weeks ago."

She started to lecture the boy, but he began to cry. Jason had headed off many a lecture that way. She hugged him and said, "Okay, here's what we'll do . . . ." She sent Jason to bed, then went to work on the project. There was no time to buy modeling clay, so she came up with a fair substitute concocted of flour and water. She drew the map on a piece of cardboard and modeled the mountains. Then, by paraphrasing an article from the encyclopedia and using Jason-like vocabulary, she wrote a paper on California history. By the time she was finished, the mountains were dry enough to paint, so she got some poster paints out of the garage and applied the colors. Then she woke her son and had him recopy the paper she had written. It was then 6 A.M.—she had worked through the night.

Jason got an A— on his California history project. And he learned a lesson that would carry him throughout his life: *If I whine and cry, Mom will always bail me out.*

Today, Jason is twenty-seven, still lives at home, and alternates between dead-end jobs and unemployment. His mother makes his meals, washes his clothes, makes excuses for him, and protects him from the big, bad, nasty world out there. She means well. She's always meant well. But she has never let her little boy grow up.

Jason's mom is a Parent Who Loves Too Much, one of a number of parental categories we will examine in this chapter and the two following chapters. Other categories include:

- **Unloving Parents**
- **Martyr Parents**
- **The Weak, Unavailable Father**
- **Dictator-Parents**
- **Parents Who Prophesied**
- **Abusive Parents**
- **Seductive Parents**

There are unique dynamics in each of these styles of parenting. In the next few pages we will see how these dynamics affected us as children and continue to affect us as adults. We will learn how the cycles of these parental styles ensnare us— and what we can do to break the cycles and build a healthy relationship, even with an emotionally unhealthy parent.

PARENTS WHO LOVE TOO MUCH

The label *Parents Who Love Too Much* was coined by Laurie Ashner and Mitch Meyerson in their book *When Parents Love Too Much* (William Morrow & Co., 1990). The phrase may sound absurd at first. After all, how can any parent love a child too much? But if you have such a parent, then you know what a painful and suffocating experience it can be to be "overparented."

This parent is characterized by intense overinvolvement, overprotectiveness, and a need to control. He overparents in order to dispel anxiety and compensate for hurts and short-comings in his own childhood. This parent becomes enmeshed in the child's life, and discourages any independent thoughts, actions, and feelings on the part of the child. Frequently, this parent will unconsciously judge the child who doesn't live up to expectations, causing the child to feel inadequate and insecure.

Outwardly, a Parent Who Loves Too Much may seem to be a Super Mom or Super Dad: very involved in the child's school activities; continually chauffering the child to music and dance lessons, sports activities, and other extracurricular events; always giving the child the best of everything—the best schools, the best clothes, the best toys, and, as they get older, the most expensive car and the biggest, most expensive wedding.

The symptoms of a Parent Who Loves Too Much begin very early in the parent/child relationship and continue to manifest themselves in adulthood. Those symptoms include:

- devoting huge blocks of lot of time and energy to activities which develop the child's abilities— helping with homework, sports activities, music and dance lessons. The Parent Who Loves Too Much is often so absorbed in the child's activities that she seems to have no life of her own.
- being obsessed with the goal of being a "good parent" and raising "good children." The Parent Who Loves Too Much constantly worries that the child may fail and that the child's failure would be perceived as his own failure as a parent.
- a reluctance to let the child out of sight for a few

hours or days. The Parent Who Loves Too Much will not go out for an evening and leave the child with a baby-sitter. This parent is also reluctant to let a child leave home for summer camp, overnight parties, or visits with friends. She sets restrictions on the child's activities. The child spends a lot of time at home, and he either misses a lot of field trips and birthday parties, or the parent always accompanies him.

The adult child of a Parent Who Loves Too Much often has problems with intimacy and relationships, thrives on the approval of others, experiences guilt (often misplaced), feels life is unfair, has difficulty trusting others, needs to feel in control, has a tendency to be self-critical, has trouble making decisions, and may be susceptible to eating disorders. This adult child has a tendency to love parents too much.

"My parents divorced when I was ten," says Ginny. "There was a big, messy custody battle, and I remember this one awful scene when both my mom and dad swore at each other, 'You'll never see those kids again!' Eventually, things simmered down. I realize now that they both must have felt terribly guilty about the divorce because they showered my sister and me with gifts—I call them 'bribes'—to get us to forgive them for breaking up our home.

"When I was sixteen, Mom bought me a car, a little red MG sports car, only two years old. When my dad found out about it, he was furious. On one of his visitation weekends, he told me he was planning to get me a 'real car' for graduation, but now that Mom had bought me that 'death trap on wheels,' he figured he better do something quick. Then he pointed to this huge brand-new Lincoln sitting in the driveway. "It's all yours,' he said. 'I want you to drive something safe, not that little red beer can.' Well, I hated that huge car, but he made me drive it home. He took my MG and sold it and sent my mom a check for what she paid for it. What a fight *that* caused."

Ginny's parents continued this pattern even after she was a married adult. "Bribing," ignoring her wishes, running her life, were all a misguided attempt to atone for their divorce when she was young. "My mom sent me presents for no reason at all," she recalls. "Very expensive presents too. Jewelry. Clothes. Expensive porcelain and crystal knicknacks for the house. 'I just thought you could use something nice,' she'd say. My dad would usually just send money. There was always a note attached, suggesting how I should spend it.

"A lot of people would say, 'Presents? Money? What is this lady complaining about?' And at first, I liked it. But I gradually realized that those gifts were intended to keep me in the position of a little girl—dependent and unable to make my way in the world. They both used those presents to control me. I finally told my Mom that if she gave me any more presents, I was going to hold a big yard sale and sell everything for a penny on the dollar. And I told my Republican father that if he sent me any more money, I was going to donate it in his name to the Democratic Party."

A child of Parents Who Love Too Much often grows up feeling:

- like a fraud: "If people knew the real me, they would reject me."
- afraid of making a mistake.
- highly self-critical—critical of her abilities, accomplishments, and appearance.
- he must always be perfect.
- she must never be shown to be wrong.
- he must suppress normal emotions, such as anger or frustration.
- she must maintain a facade: "Everything's fine. I don't have any problems," even when her entire world is coming unglued.

Many Parents Who Love Too Much *know* (or at least *sense*) that they are hurting their children by overparenting them, but they are almost helpless to stop themselves. As one Mother Who Loves Too Much told me, "I pick up my kids from school, throw them into the station wagon, drag them to soccer practice and dance lessons and voice and piano lessons, then I drag them home and throw them in their rooms and nag and browbeat them about their homework until they're crying. If they don't win the Principal's Trophy or if they miss a soccer goal or if they flub one note at the recital, I take them home and scream at them. I hate myself for it—but I can't stop myself, either."

Here are some strategies for dealing with the emotional aftermath of an overparented childhood and for drawing healthy boundary lines in your ongoing relationship with a Parent Who Loves Too Much:

Practice ignoring the inner critic. Don't listen to the voice that tells you that you must be perfect, that you are inadequate in your abilities or personal appearance.

Take risks in your life, your career, and your relationships. Dare to make changes based on what you want from life, not on what your parents want for you. Dare to be honest with others, including your parents, about what you want and what you feel. If you feel anger or hurt over something they have done, take the risk of telling them, but avoid doing so in a hostile or hysterical way. If you have been raised to think that you aren't talented or capable or if you've been taught to always play it safe, then challenge yourself to take on some new risk every day. Reach out to someone you don't know, such as a neighbor or coworker, and make a new friend.

Remember that no one—not even a parent—can control you if you don't allow it. Be proactive. Be your own person. Act, don't just react.

Draw some boundary lines in your life and tell your parents where those boundary lines lie. If you don't like your parents snooping in your refrigerator to see if you're eating right, or asking questions about your sex life, or dropping by without phoning, then draw a line around that area. When your parent crosses that line, politely but firmly explain that this is an area you consider private, and you want your privacy respected in that area. Your parent may disagree with you or act hurt when you set limits, so be prepared and avoid getting drawn into an argument or manipulative games. Tell your parent, "I understand how you feel and that you don't like the limits I'm setting, but these are the limits I need for my own well-being, and I hope you'll try to understand my feelings and my needs." Whatever your parent says in response, just bring it back to this one simple statement and don't get drawn into a point-by-point debate.

If you are accepting money from an enmeshed parent and find it difficult not to accept it, set a deadline for "cutting the cord" of financial dependence upon your parents. Give yourself three to six months to make the transition to a tighter budget and share this deadline with a trusted friend or counselor who can hold you accountable to keep this commitment to yourself and your parents.

Stay within your own boundary lines. Some adult children find it hard to break out of the enmeshment pattern. They unwittingly invite their parents to cross the boundary lines by volunteering information. They talk about problems at work, even though they know it will trigger unwanted career advice. They say things like, "I haven't been getting much sleep lately," even though they know it will trigger nagging and advice-giving. Why do people do it? While some adult children hate the enmeshment and overparenting on one level, on another level they crave it: "Please nurture me and take care of me again! I can't handle the freedom of being a full-fledged adult!" Avoid falling into this trap.

Understand that as you try to draw appropriate boundaries in your relationship with your parents, they will object. They may scream and cry and carry on. If they are enmeshed in your life, they may claim you are killing them, that they cannot live without the overinvolved relationship they have had with you. But they will survive. Everyone feels angry, sad, hurt, lonely, scared, or depressed at times, and everybody survives it.

Accept the fact that your parents will eventually die. If they use their mortality as a manipulative tool against you ("You're sending us to an early grave!"), just realize that manipulation is all it is. Sure, they will eventually die, but not because you have taken a perfectly reasonable and necessary step toward emotional health. When they die, it will be because of a clogged artery or a weak blood vessel or a disease or a truck they didn't see—but it won't be because you decided to change an unhealthy relationship.

Lila is a Mother Who Loves Too Much. She always pushed her daughter Emily to achieve and excel, to be the class president, to be a cheerleader, to be the valedictorian. By age seventeen, Emily had an ulcer and was plagued with severe bouts of depression. She married at age twenty-one—the wedding rivaled that of Charles and Diana—and she was divorced at age twenty-four. Emily's husband said that the reason he didn't want to be married anymore was the relentless perfectionism of Emily *and her mother.* Lila continually intruded in their lives during the brief span of their marriage, telling them how to decorate their house, telling them how to budget their money, telling them how to plan their family (including bedroom advice), and giving them both career and financial advice.

'It wasn't just that Mom told me what to do and what to think," Emily recalls, "but she wouldn't even listen to me. Mom is a strict teetotaler, so when she saw a bottle of wine in my refrigerator, she said, 'Emily, what's this doing in here? You don't drink wine!' I said, 'Mom, I like a glass with dinner now and then.' She said, 'Emily, you do *not* drink wine! I raised you better than that!' If I voice an idea in religion or politics that differs from hers, she smiles patronizingly and says, 'Oh, you don't really believe that.' I can't get through to her."

Once during an argument, Emily let it slip that she was in counseling. Lila went ballistic: "Are you telling some stranger that I was a bad parent?!" She demanded to talk to me, to give me "her side." So, with Emily's permission, I met with Lila.

"I've been a *good* mother to that girl," Lila told me. "I've given her all the love any child could want." I assured her that Emily had never for a moment questioned her mother's love. Emily just wanted a healthy boundary line between her mother's life and her own. At this, Lila became very angry. She accused me of undermining her relationship with Lila. She underscored the love she had showered on Emily: She had breastfed Emily until she was three. She had never left Emily with baby-sitters, because no sitter met Lila's high standards. She had given Emily every advantage a child could want. Lila knew what it was like to have an unloving, neglectful mother, and she had made absolutely sure that Emily would never lack love and affection as she herself had.

In short, everything Lila said was an unwitting admission of how enmeshed she was in Emily's life, and why. By over-mothering Emily, she was overcompensating for the lack of mothering in her own childhood. In a real sense, she was actually re-mothering herself, vicariously feeding on the over-abundant love she gave Emily. Lila and I met several more times, and I tried to mirror back what she was saying so that she could hear it from Emily's perspective. But Lila eventually quit coming and was never able to see any needs or any perspective except her own. To Lila, Emily was an ungrateful child who should have been *overjoyed* to receive all the love and attention that Lila never got from her own mother.

Fortunately, Emily was able to acquire the coping skills to deal effectively with a mother who was not going to change. She was able to build a fence between herself and her mother's intrusive love. It is a fence with a gate, so she can let her mother in whenever she chooses, but the gate has a lock, and Emily has the key.

If you have a Parent Who Loves Too Much, you can build the same protective fence around your life that Emily did. But perhaps your problem was not being overparented, but being tragically underparented. Perhaps the parents you struggle with are unloving parents.

UNLOVING PARENTS

"Everybody always told me how lucky I was to have a dad like him," Eric recalls. "'A model father,' they called him. Oh, he's a 'model' all right, just like the model airplane kits you buy at the hobby shop—all plastic and hollow inside.

"Dad was a politician, a real big-shot in the state assembly. He was preaching 'family values' before anyone ever heard of Dan Quayle. He really cultivated an image as a family man, and I remember how our whole family would pose for publicity shots and TV ads for his campaigns. It was always real confusing for me, the way he preached so much about the importance of the family, about raising kids in a loving home, because I never really knew if he loved me or not. Whenever the cameras were clicking or there was an audience, he was the perfect father, and everyone would tell me what a super dad I had. But when there were no spectators, he didn't even know I was alive.

Eric's father was like many unloving parents: He had a reputation as a "model father," and he played that role to the hilt. His performance in the role of "model father" enhanced his public reputation and helped win elections, but children are not fooled by a performance. For much of his life, Eric was painfully aware of the dissonance between his father's image and the evidence of his own feelings: "My dad was like a puzzle in which the pieces didn't fit," Eric recalls. "I was never able to make sense of this man until I went into counseling and found out about the *narcissistic personality disorder.*"

In Greek mythology, Narcissus was the handsome son of a river god and a nymph. Looking into the waters of a spring, he fell in love with his own reflection and remained there, absorbed in his own image, until he wasted away. His self-absorption was his undoing. It is easy to see why people who are pathologically self-absorbed are called *narcissists.* Tragically, people with the narcissistic personality disorder tend to be the undoing not only of themselves but also of their children.

Narcissists are virtually incapable of giving love; they are even incapable of *learning* how to love. Narcissists think of themselves as wonderful people, and narcissistic parents often view themselves as perfect parents. Yet they don't really understand what love is. Understand, we are not talking here about an *abusive* parent, the kind who molests or beats a child. We are talking about a parent who generally provides all the basic necessities of life except *attention* and *affection.*

Many children and adolescents pass through relatively harmless stages of juvenile narcissism on their way to healthy adulthood. But narcissism in adults is a destructive aberration. Some psychoanalysts, such as M. Scott Peck and Erich Fromm, use the term "malignant narcissism" to describe this personality problem, a term which suggests a disorder that is harmful and cancerous by nature.

Barbara is the daughter of a narcissistic mother. She doesn't remember a single time in her life when her mother ever hugged her or said, "I love you," nor does she remember any time when her mother ever struck her, not even a spanking. It was as if there was no contact, no touch, no feeling at all in their relationship.

"My mother fancied herself an artist, a painter and a sculptor," Barbara recalls. "She showed her work in some local galleries, but she never went very far. It's not that she didn't have plenty of time to create. My dad earned enough so that mother didn't have to work. In fact, they always hired an *au pair* so that mother didn't even have to be bothered with taking care of me.

"When I was growing up, there were a couple times I asked her, 'Mother, do you really love me?' And she'd say, 'What a silly question. What mother wouldn't love her own child?' But she'd never just say, 'Yes, Barbara, I love you.' One time when I was eleven or twelve, I overheard an argument between her and Daddy. I remember it vividly because they were arguing about me. Daddy wanted to take me with them on a trip, and she wanted to leave me with a sitter. And I'll never forget one thing she said to Daddy: 'Why do I have to change my plans for Barbara? Barbara is just an accident that happened in the back seat of your convertible when I was nineteen years old.' That's when I really knew how she felt about me."

Some parents are so blatantly unloving that the child does not have to wonder if he or she is loved or not: being unloved is a cruel but obvious fact of life. The parent may even berate the child and say, "I never wanted you! I'd be better off without you! You've ruined my life!" The child adjusts to this situation by assuming that all parents are unloving and that all children have to put up with feeling unwanted and even hated by their parents.

But most narcissists are much more subtle and deceptive about their unloving nature. They put out mixed signals, saying "I love you" with their words and "I don't love you" with their actions. So the children of narcissistic parents often grow up like Eric, with a deep sense of confusion and a low estimation of their own worth.

The dominant feature of a narcissistic personality is extreme self-centeredness and self-absorption (though many narcissists convincingly pose as warm, caring people). The narcissist has a grandiose, exaggerated estimate of her abilities and often fantasizes a life of great fame, wealth, power, and idealized romantic love. The narcissist is usually a person of insatiable ambition, though she is not always realistic about reaching those goals. This person constantly feeds on attention and admiration and is more concerned about appearances than reality.

Although narcissistic personalities can be found in all walks of life, there are certain professions which seem to attract an excessively large proportion of narcissists: politics, the fine arts, the performing arts (such as acting or music), and—most tragic of all—the ministry. (Most pastors, of course, are committed, sincere people who feel called by God to serve Him on a full-time basis. But it is important to note there are some who inhabit the role of pastor because it affords an excellent disguise.) The reasons these professions attract narcissists is not hard to find, for these are *roles* which can allow the narcissist to craft a public persona and attract public applause. He or she can wrap this idealized image around the hollow reality of his or her personality, and thus conceal the truth from others and from himself.

Narcissists have little or no empathy for other people's feelings or needs and typically display an attitude of entitlement. They expect favors from other people but feel no responsibility to reciprocate. Narcissists routinely exploit other people, including friends and relations, and they often do so in such subtle and manipulative ways that people don't even know they are being used. To the narcissist, other people (including his own family) exist to meet his needs and gratify his wants. When people fail to act according to his wishes and expectations, he is astonished and often becomes very angry.

For example, Eric vividly remembers his father pushing him to go out for basketball in high school. "I told my dad, 'I'm not going out for basketball. I'm not good at it, and besides, I don't even like basketball.' He looked at me strangely and said, 'Of course, you like basketball. I was great at basketball.' I thought to myself, 'What am I missing here? He was a star center in high school, so *that* means *I* have to love the

game? Non sequitur, man! Tilt! Where's the logic in that?'"
What Eric now knows but didn't understand at the time is
that it is very common for a narcissist to project his own beliefs, experiences, and feelings on other people and expect
them to act according to his wishes. The narcissist is so self-
centered that he sees other people not as distinct individuals
but as extensions of himself.

Now we begin to see why the narcissistic personality disorder produces such completely unloving parents. Feeling that
the world should be ordered to meet their needs, they feel
deeply imposed upon and resentful if they are asked to meet
someone else's needs—*even the needs of their own children.*
Eric's mother reports that her husband never changed a dia-
per, never gave Eric a bath, never lifted a finger with any of
the parental chores.

"Once," she recalls, "when Eric was about three, he and I
both came down with a terrible flu at the same time. I was in
no condition to care for a sick child, yet Eric's father never did
a single thing to help us. He was right there in the house, just
a few steps down the hall, but he couldn't be bothered with a
sick family because he was writing a speech for a party fund-
raiser. The speech was three whole weeks away, but he
couldn't even spare ten seconds to come down the hall and
see if Eric and I were alive or dead."

Narcissists exhibit an intense preoccupation with grooming, exercising, and dressing their bodies. They are obsessed
with staying youthful and being attractive to the opposite sex.
They also worry constantly about their health and are quick to
take every ache, twinge, and digestive problem to a doctor.
Narcissists often talk to others about their body functions and
malfunctions (including their various lumps, rashes, and
bowel movements) so that others will be worried for them too.

For narcissists, sex is not about closeness and intimacy but
is merely another expression of their preoccupation with
their own self-importance. Narcissists frequently enjoy
wielding sex as a weapon of power; they seduce and they con-

quer and they exploit, but they have little interest in giving pleasure to another human being. Whereas the God-given gift of sexuality is about sharing and giving, narcissism is about taking.

One of the most troubling features of narcissistic personalities is that they are expert liars—*and they frequently don't even know it!* Their perception of reality is highly fluid. If reality does not suit their self-aggrandizing purposes, they simply edit the facts in their own mind. The biggest lie of most narcissists is the lie regarding *who they see themselves to be*. They often cultivate an external image of caring, selfless, morally superior people when the inner reality is quite the opposite. That is why M. Scott Peck calls them (in his book of the same title) *People of the Lie*. He writes:

> Utterly dedicated to preserving their self-image of perfection, they are unceasingly engaged in the effort to maintain the appearance of moral purity. They worry about this a great deal. . . . While they seem to lack any motivation to *be* good, they intensely desire to *appear* good. Their "goodness" is all on a level of pretense. It is, in effect, a lie. . . . The lie is designed not so much to deceive others as to deceive themselves.[1]

The narcissist will lie or rationalize to cover up mistakes, character defects, or harm he has caused other people. He will also fake emotions, such as caring or sympathy, in order to impress other people and maintain his image as a good person.

You put all of these factors together, and the net result is a person who is unable to love, unable to have an honest, intimate relationship with another person. He cannot truly love a spouse or a child. He cannot emotionally nurture another person. Children need love, and love is the one thing narcissists cannot provide.

What happens, then, to the unloved children of narcissistic parents? The effects are tragic and profound:

The unloved child grows up feeling he is an intrusion on his parent's life. In many cases, the narcissistic parent never wanted the child in the first place. The child might have been unplanned or the birth may have created a financial or career hardship or a social embarrassment. So there may be active resentment toward the child on the part of the narcisstic parent, which the parent communicates to the child in many ways.

Being unloved and ignored leaves a child (including an adult child) feeling unlovable and without value. If you were unloved as a child, you probably have great difficulty loving yourself. You may experience feelings of being inadequate, inept, unattractive, and without value.

Adult children of narcissistic parents are frequently bent on finding the love and attention they missed in childhood. This obsession tends to dominate their romantic relationships. Ironically, adult children of unloving parents tend to seek out unloving people as marriage partners! The reason: they unconsciously gravitate toward people who symbolically represent that unloving, narcissistic parent so that they can continue the no-win struggle for Mom's or Dad's nonexistent affection. The result is that the adult child ends up being revictimized by unloving people again and again.

Sons of narcissistic mothers spend their childhood and adolescence trying to coax an unloving mother into demonstrating affection. Then, as adults, they frequently replay the same scenario with the women in their lives. Often, they will unconsciously take revenge against an unloving mother by punishing other women, frequently using sex as a weapon.

Daughters of narcissistic mothers often turn to other people in adulthood to find the love and mothering they missed in childhood. They may seek "mothering" from men or from other women. (Current research suggests that narcissistic mothers may play a part in tilting some women toward lesbianism.)

Sons of narcissistic fathers respond to being unloved in various ways. Those who were disparaged and demeaned by a cruel narcissistic father often become passive adults, having accepted Dad's repeated message that they are worthless. Other sons respond by attaching themselves to Mom, either by becoming very enmeshed and dependent upon Mom or becoming locked into a spiraling conflict cycle with her. (To the unconscious mind, any sign of parental involvement is better than being ignored, so if a child can't obtain loving attention, he will settle for *angry* attention.)

Children of narcissistic parents often copy their parents' narcissistic tendencies. In particular, sons often copy the narcissistic personalities of their fathers, becoming as adept at exploiting, seducing, and manipulating others as Dad was.

Daughters of narcissistic fathers struggle with a sense of being unlovely and unlovable. "If my own father didn't love me," they think, "how can any man love me?" Daughters of unloving fathers tend to be drawn into relationships with unloving men, where they are exploited and the message "You are unlovable" is again reinforced. Such women continually try to please and accommodate their partners, vainly trying to win a love that does not exist.

Salli is the daughter of a narcissistic father. She is an attractive young woman, but there was a time when you couldn't tell her that. "My eyes are too large, and I'm too tall," she would say, even though her eyes are strikingly beautiful and her height is only five foot nine. Unloved by her father, Salli decided that no man would ever love her. So whenever a man showed interest in her, she was so flattered and desperate to win his affection that she would throw herself at him and allow herself to be sexually exploited. In the process, she gained a reputation around her office for being "easy."

Salli needed to understand three things: her promiscuous

lifestyle was sinful and self-destructive; her desperate search for love was actually motivated by low self-esteem, caused by an unloving father; and by making herself available to so many men, she was ruining her chances of finding real love.

Armed with these insights, Salli was able to make changes in her behavior and in her image of herself. She still has a lot of healing ahead of her, but she has taken a major step. In the words of the once popular song, Salli is no longer "looking for love in all the wrong places."

If you are the adult child of a narcissistic parent, then you must face this fact: your narcissistic parent never loved you and probably never will. This is *not* because of any defect in you. Your unloving parent has always been *incapable* of loving anyone, including you. There is nothing you can do to win his love—*nothing*. While I would never say that anyone is "incurable"—particularly since I believe in the power of God to heal both the body and the soul—the narcissistic personality disorder is as close to an incurable condition as there is.

Why is it so difficult for a narcissist to change? One reason is that the disorder is such a fundamental part of that person's psychological makeup. Narcissism is not what a person thinks, believes, or feels. It is not a chemical imbalance that can be treated with drugs. It is not something a person "has" but *who a person is*. To "cure" such a person, you would practically have to rip out the old personality and install a completely new one.

Another reason narcissists rarely change is that they are so adept at rearranging reality to suit themselves. No matter how you try to rub their noses in the truth, you cannot convince them that they have a problem. The truth slides off them like water off a duck's back.

So, if you are the child of a narcissist, your energies are better spent in focusing on your healing, rebuilding your self-esteem, and enhancing your capacity to give and receive love in a healthy relationship. A counselor or therapist can help you find the insight you need to form healthy relationships with people who know how to love.

That is the path Eric has chosen follow in his search for wholeness. "I've decided," he concludes, "that even if my dad never loved me, I can love myself and receive love and validation from God. No matter what kind of person my dad has been, I'm going to be a *whole* person."

And you can be a whole person, too. In the next few chapters, we will examine practical steps you can take to find God's loving validation and the courage to live a secure and healthy life, regardless of how you have been loved or unloved by your parents.

5

Parenting Styles That Hinder Healthy Relationships

"**M**y mother's name is Joanne," says Susan. "My husband Lee calls her 'Joanne of Arc' because she's such a martyr. It wasn't until after I married Lee that I realized what my mother has been doing to me. I thought it was normal for a child to grow up feeling guilty all the time. But after getting to know Lee's parents, I realized that not all parents are like my mom.

"It goes back as long as I can remember. Mom had a real hard pregnancy. She had to spend the last two months of it flat on her back in bed; then she spent twenty-four hours in labor, after which they ended up delivering me by caesarean section. She must have told me that story a dozen times, from the time I was little until just the other day. And when she used to tell me that, I would feel awful about all the pain and inconvenience I caused my mother. Then, when the guilt would start to throb inside my chest almost harder than I could stand, she would add, 'But I would go through it all over again for you, dear. That's what a mother's love is all about.'

"Whenever I forgot one of my chores or did something wrong, it was always, 'After all I've suffered for you, I'd think you could do one little thing for me.' And it always worked. This pattern continued right on into my adulthood. When she was in the hospital for her gall bladder surgery, I visited her twice a day, but she made me feel terrible for all the hours she had to be there with no one to complain to. She told me how mean the nurses were and how much pain she was in, and then she'd top it off with, 'But I guess that's why the Lord has allowed so much pain in my life, to teach me to bear it alone.'

"She continually hinted to me that she wasn't going to be around for long. 'The doctor told me I need another operation,' she'd say. 'But I figure, Why keep patching a tire that doesn't have any tread left? I'm ready to meet the Lord, and nobody here will miss me anyway.' And, of course, I was expected to leap in and assure her that, yes, everybody loves her and she's got plenty of years to go and we need her and on and on and on.

"Last year, Lee and I planned a two-week vacation in Hawaii. We had never been to Hawaii before, and we had never really had the honeymoon we wanted, so we decided to leave the kids with Lee's folks and take off, just the two of us. When I told my mother about our vacation plans, she said, 'I'm happy for you,' but she said it in a tone that meant, 'So, you're going to go off and leaving a dying old lady all alone, huh?' And then she added, 'Well, I suppose I'll see you when you get back.' I said, 'Of course you will.' She shrugged and said, 'I don't know. I've been having these heart palpitations . . . But you kids deserve a nice time. I've heard Hawaii is just beautiful. I've always wanted to go there, but your father and I could never afford it, with all my medical bills and raising you and all. I'm just glad that you and Lee can afford a nice vacation like that. So don't you worry about me. No matter what happens, just remember the Lord is with me.'

"Obviously, she wanted to go to Hawaii with us. I felt so guilty that I went home and told Lee we needed to take

Mother with us. Well, Lee just hit the roof! 'We have two round-trip tickets and a reservation for two at the resort,' he said, 'so if you want to take your mother to Hawaii like a good, guilty little girl, then bon voyage and aloha, I hope the two of you have a nice time! But I am *not* going to spend two weeks in paradise with Joanne of Arc!' 'Well, what should I do?' I said. I really felt trapped. Lee said, 'What you should do, Susan, is grow up! Tell your mother she can't jerk you around anymore! Tell her you won't give in to emotional blackmail anymore! Tell her this is *our* vacation, not hers!'

"I was horrified. I said, 'I can't tell her that! It would kill her! I love my mother!' He said, 'I know you do, and you should love her. But you can't let her manipulate you with guilt anymore.' Lee was right, but I still didn't know what to do."

MARTYR PARENTS

Susan had grown up with a Martyr Parent. A Martyr Parent uses guilt to control her child. Martyr Parents are commonly satirized on TV and in movies. (In the sitcom *Rhoda*, Rhoda's mother, Ida Morgenstern, is a classic example). They can be fun to watch on the screen, but they are miserable to live with. The genius of Martyr Parents is that they don't have to get their way in order to win. They just bear their suffering stoically and loudly: "Fine. Ignore me. Do what you want. I'm only your mother." Or, "My feelings never mattered to you anyway. I'm only your father." As Erma Bombeck has said, "Guilt is the gift that keeps on giving."

Martyr Parents use their own misery (real, feigned, or imagined) as a bit in your mouth and a spur to your backside. With guilt, they can control all your movements: prod you forward, turn you to the right or the left, or pull you up short like any well-trained horse. Equally tragic, children of Martyr Parents often replay the familiar scenario by yoking themselves with Martyr Mates or by becoming Martyr Parents themselves. The results can range from marital conflict to sexual dysfunction to perpetuating the same cycle with their own children.

What causes people to become Martyr Parents? The factors include:

- *Culture and family tradition.*   In many families, Martyr Parenting is passed down from generation to generation. Your grandparents controlled your parent with guilt, and your parent now controls you with guilt. If you don't find a way to break the cycle, you may find yourself passing this charming little tradition on to your own children.
- *Low self-esteem.*   Your Martyr Parent has grown up feeling unlovable. He reasons that since no one could ever respond to him out of love and respect, he must use suffering and guilt to get his way.
- *Martyrdom effectiveness.*   Your Martyr Parent says, "Meet my needs. Do what I say. Pay attention to me—or I will get sick or cry or moan or even die! And then how will you feel?" So you respond. You grit your teeth, you hate yourself for it, but you respond. And every time you respond, you reinforce the idea in your parent's mind that *martyrdom pays*.

How, then, do you respond to a Martyr Parent without being controlled?

First, stop enabling your Martyr Parent's behavior. Easier said than done, right? Of course it is. But the fact is that every time you give in to manipulation guilt, you are *willingly participating* in your parent's unhealthy behavior pattern. You *do* have a choice. Yes, you are being strongly pressured to make a different choice by your Martyr Parent, but your parent can't *force* you to do what she demands. If your parent controls your actions, it is because you have surrendered your will.

It takes a lot of insight, strength, and courage to take a stand against a controlling Martyr Parent. When a parent goes into the martyr routine, he is really *threatening* you: "I will be angry with you. I will blame you. I won't love you anymore." These are powerful messages, and they generate feelings of anxiety and fear that are hard to resist. But if you stand your ground, you will gradually learn that you *can* survive these confrontations—and so can your Martyr Parent.

Second, refuse to play the game. Remember the chess analogy from chapter 1: Your parent makes a move, you make a countermove, your parent counters your move—and there is a predictable pattern to all these moves. But you can break out of that pattern and end the game. Normally, when your parent makes a "move," you respond with an almost prearranged response. Your parent makes a statement that says, "Do what I want, or I will suffer because of your selfishness." Your usual response may be to feel twisted with guilt inside and to give in to your parent's demand. Or your usual response may be to whine or argue or accuse your parent. Or your usual response may be to attempt to countermanipulate your parent with some guilt of your own.

Whatever your usual response, the next time your parent opens the game with the guilt gambit, try a *different* response. Tell your parent, "I'm choosing not to do what you want. That doesn't mean that I'm selfish or ungrateful or that I don't love you. In fact, it is because of my love for you that I'm choosing not to do this. I've thought about it very carefully, and I've decided that it's not in your best interests or mine for me to do what you want."

Understand, this move won't end the game. Your parent still has plenty of moves at his disposal. Your parent will tell you how unjust you are being and may even recite a whole laundry list of your injustices. Prepare for whining and crying and complaints about your cruelty to a parent who has never done anything but suffer for your sake. Prepare for strange, desperate behavior you have never dealt with before.

Prepare to see your Martyr Parent withdraw into a sullen silence, maybe into a grudge lasting days or weeks.

But whatever you do, don't get drawn into the game. Just keep returning to your original statement and keep reinforcing it: "I know you feel I am not being fair or compassionate. I hope you'll trust me that I'm making this choice because I love you and because this is in your best interests and mine. But whether you accept my decision or not, I am still going to do what I think is right."

If you stay with the same message—a message that says your decision is firm and unshakable but guided by love and respect for your parent—then you can't be pulled off course, you can't be diverted into unproductive arguments on side issues.

Third, recognize that you cannot be the answer to all your Martyr Parent's problems and needs. You cannot make your parent happy or heal your parent's sorrow or keep your parent alive forever. You can't make up for the deficits and pain in your Martyr Parent's upbringing. Recognize that you don't have to continually prove and re-prove your love to your parent by continuing to be controlled by him.

These are the lessons Susan had to learn in dealing with her Martyr Mother, "Joanne of Arc." Fortunately, she did learn, and she did so in time to save her Hawaiian honeymoon. "I had another talk with Mother," she recalls. "It was very hard, and I needed the help of a counselor to give me the insight and the strategies to feel confident enough to attempt it. I told Mother I loved her but that this trip was for Lee and me. I told her that someday we would take her on a family vacation somewhere. She responded—as I knew she would— 'Sometimes someday never comes. You know, Susan, nobody lasts forever.' I said, 'Well, Mom, I'm sure you'll be fine until Lee and I get back from Hawaii, but like you said, no matter what happens, the Lord will be with you.' She looked at me with eyes as big as saucers, but she didn't know what to say! I had taken her heaviest artillery, that old threat of 'Do what I say or I may just up and die!' and I had completely disarmed it!

"Before Lee and I left on vacation, Mother told me to call her a few times from Hawaii. I said, 'I'll send you some post-cards.' And that's exactly what I did. Lee and I had a wonderful time together. It was the best two weeks of my life. And that was the turning point in my relationship with Joanne of Arc. She still tries to pull the old martyr routine from time to time, but she's a lot less dependent than she used to be. I think she's figured out that even though she can't control me like she used to, I still love her. And that will never change."

THE WEAK, UNAVAILABLE FATHER

"My dad was a clerk for the country public works department," says Aaron. "When I was about fourteen, one of the women in my dad's office sued him for child support. She claimed my dad fathered her baby. Well, I just knew that couldn't be true, because I'd met this woman—she worked at the counter right next to my dad. She was the most dimwitted, unkempt, unattractive woman I had ever seen. No way would my dad ever risk losing a terrific woman like my mother over someone like that!

"Dad denied everything, and we all believed him and rallied around him. He told us that the woman had a history of psychiatric problems. He kept referring to her as 'that mentally defective woman.' Well, the court ordered a paternity test, and my dad got real agitated about that. Finally, he and Mom had this huge fight. They closed the doors, but my sister and I could hear every word. My mom was hitting my dad and screaming at him to get out of the house. He was pleading and crying, and finally he left. I never saw him again. He just disappeared. I knew he was really gone for good about two months later when my mom had a yard sale and sold all his clothes."

Aaron vividly remembers the shame of that experience. "Everybody knew what my father had done," he recalls. "People were always talking about it, especially the people in my church. My friends at school pulled back from me. Everybody knew. That was fifteen years ago, and there isn't a day goes by that I don't remember the shame my dad brought on my family."

Every child wants to grow up feeling that Dad is the strongest, bravest, most competent father in the world. Every child wants Dad to be the one who leads the way to happiness, wisdom, and security. So there are few more painful experiences in life than the discovery that Dad is weak, ineffectual, and unavailable.

A child can be proud of a father who makes mistakes. Or who has been beaten up and knocked around by the world. Or who has given his best effort yet failed in business. Or who cries when overwhelmed by grief or joy or patriotism. There is no shame in any of these things.

But how can a child be proud of a father who has no character or integrity? Who has no courage? Who never takes a stand for himself or anyone else? Who brings shame on his family? Who lets himself be dominated by other people, including his wife? Who is withdrawn and absorbed in meaningless pastimes—drinking, gambling, television, sleeping—rather than being involved with his own family? A Weak, Unavailable Father may take any of the following forms:

- A man who surrenders his will, his opinions, and his rights to a domineering wife. The stereotype of this man is a passive wimp. But he may also be a man who is in continual conflict with his wife—perhaps even a violent, raging conflict—but who always surrenders in the end.
- A man who is dominated by compulsions or addictions such as drug addiction, alcoholism, sexual addiction, or gambling.

- A man who has no opinions, no preferences, no ambitions, no will of his own. If offered a choice by his wife, his boss, or by the world in general, his response is "It doesn't matter to me. Whatever you say is fine with me."

- A man who seldom disciplines in his own right or according to his own principles but punishes his children in his wife's name and at her bidding. He has abdicated the parenting role.

- A man who can't handle his own feelings or the feelings of others. A man who withdraws from expressions of affection and from expressions of anger; a man whose weakness is displayed in the form of a brittle temper, who flies into a rage or a tantrum when others disagree with him. (The ability to express and receive honest emotions is part of a man's strength. The impairment of that capacity is a weakness.)

- A man who is unavailable as a source of guidance and fatherly advice. If a father has no values, character, or ambition, why would a child turn to him for help with a problem or a decision? A Weak, Unavailable Father has no counsel to offer on such subjects as career choices, peer pressure, dating, ethical decisions, or coping with friends and enemies on the schoolyard.

Abby's most vivid memory of her father is one of shame and disgust. Her mother was a narcissistic playgirl who was flagrant about her affairs with other men. Her father was a weak, dependent man who actually stepped aside and allowed his wife to bring her boyfriends into their bedroom. "Years later, I asked my dad why he allowed that to go on," Abby recalls. "He just looked at me with this big question mark on his face and said, 'What could I do?' I wanted to tell him he should have thrown those men out of his bedroom and given my mother an ultimatum, but he looked so pathetic, I just couldn't say it."

The effect of Weak, Unavailable Fathers on their children is profound and reaches far into adulthood. Here are some examples of how children are affected:

Both sons and daughters of Weak, Unavailable Fathers are left with serious deficits in their sense of security and self-confidence. Our fathers have a major role in shaping our image of ourselves. If we see Dad as a man who was weak and ineffectual, then our own strength and competence is called into question.

The adult daughter of a Weak, Unavailable Father often seeks out relationships with weak, unavailable men: men who are addicted, who lack ambition and motivation, who are unassertive, who are ill at ease with emotion, or who are willing to be dominated. This daughter has an unconscious urge to replay the past in hope of writing a different ending to the story. She seeks to reshape and rescue her symbolic Daddy and make him into the strong man her real father never was. It is a no-win struggle, destined to end in hurt and disappointment.

Tammy was nine when her father crumbled right before her eyes. "For days, I had known that something terrible had happened," she says, "but I didn't know what it was. Mom was angry with Dad, that much was obvious—but why? It was summertime, and I was home from school, and all of a sudden, Dad was home too. He wasn't going to work at the bank every day liked he used to. I thought it was strange, but I was afraid to ask what was going on.

"I went out one morning to play outside, and the newspaper was on the front step. My dad's picture was right there on the front page. The story said he was being indicted for embezzling money from the bank. I sat on the front step and read the whole article, then I went inside and put the paper in front of him, and I said, 'Daddy, is this true?' And he began to cry.

"I loved him and pitied him and despised him at the same time. A kid should never be put in the position of having to pity her father. That was the rottenest moment of my entire life."

Here are some strategies for responding to a Weak, Unavailable Father and the emotional legacy he has left in your life:

Try to understand why your father is weak and ineffectual. Sometime in his life, almost certainly at an early age, his self-confidence was stunted. Perhaps as a schoolboy, he was one of those friendless kids who spends recess walking alone by the chain link fence or being picked on by the other boys. He didn't choose to be weak, he just somehow never learned how to be strong. By understanding him, you may be able to find more compassion for him.

Try to find areas of strength in your Weak, Unavailable Father. Try to connect with those areas and affirm those strengths in him. Sometimes, you can bridge from an area of strength to an area of weakness and encourage him to strengthen that weak area. You can say, for example: "Dad, it took a lot of strength for you to go through that awful divorce. It wasn't easy, but you survived it. I think you've proven that you're strong enough to give up drinking too."

Find areas of strength within yourself. Focus and build on those strengths. Concentrate on being a person of moral, ethical, and spiritual integrity. Build courage by taking risks. Build persistence by sticking to your goals and ambitions. Build conviction by defining your opinions and core beliefs and trying to put those opinions and beliefs into practice in tangible ways.

When making friends and building relationships, be conscious and deliberate about choosing people of strength as your friends and role models. Find people who are not trapped in addictions, people who have strong convictions and moral strength, people who have a sense of direction in their lives, people who are proactive rather than passive, people who are not threatened by honest emotions.

Find a mentor—a wise, fatherly person—in your church, your support group, your Bible study group, or your office. Look for someone who can provide you the character model, insight, and guidance you need to approach life with spiritual and moral courage. Seek out strong people who can share their strength with you.

Art remembers watching his mother scream and hit his father. "They would usually fight about money," he says, "although you couldn't really call it a fight. Dad would never fight back. He'd never even talk back. He made a fairly decent living, actually, but my mom was a major spendaholic, so our family was always in hock. She'd come storming into the living room while my dad was watching TV or reading the paper, and she'd demand to know what he did with the credit cards and the checkbook. Of course, he had hidden them because the well was completely dry. So she'd scream at him, take her shoes off, and beat him with the heels. He'd just put his arms up and cover his face until she ran out of steam.

"After it was all over, he'd come to me and say, 'Art, I know this is hard for you to understand, but there's nothing else I can do. I mean, I was raised never to hit a woman.' I'd say, 'Sure, Dad, I understand.' But I didn't understand. And I still don't. He didn't have to hit her, but at least he could have stood up to her."

Perhaps the most important thing to remember about a Weak, Unavailable Father is that there is no way to pump him full of character and strength. It took many years to shape him into what he is today, and you do not have the power to turn him into something he is not. Stop struggling with him and trying to change him.

Instead, concentrate on your own issues, on your own needs, and on making *yourself* strong and available to the people who need your love and guidance. You can't remake the past, but you can prepare yourself to be strong enough to face the future.

DICTATOR-PARENTS

Dirk is the son of a Marine colonel. This colonel ran his family like a Marine platoon, with strict discipline given and strict obedience required. Colonel Dad never showed any affection or empathy for his two sons, but he did exercise an iron hand of control. He groomed his two sons to be Marine officers. He conducted inspections of the boys' bedrooms as if he were inspecting a barracks. He even bounced a quarter on the beds to make sure the blankets were taut.

Dirk and his brother Dan responded to their Dictator-Father in contrasting ways. Dan followed in his father's footsteps and was a Marine lieutenant when he was killed in Quang Tri Province, Vietnam, in 1972. Dirk was a student and antiwar activist at U.C. Santa Barbara when he learned of his brother's death. Now in his early forties, Dirk experienced a lot of confusion in his sexual identity throughout his life. Though he is married today and does not practice a gay lifestyle, he privately admits to having homosexual tendencies and fantasies and has had homosexual relationships in the past.

"My brother Dan submitted to Pop's control," Dirk recalls bitterly. "He joined Pop's team, *Semper Fi* all the way. And just look where it got him. I went the other way. I rebelled. I'm not sure, but perhaps even the homosexual feelings I have are a form of rebellion, a way of getting even, a way of setting myself apart from him, a way of escaping his control. Sometimes it hits me that my entire life has been a reaction against Pop and all he's done to me. And then I just boil over with anger, and the anger has nowhere to go because I can't talk to Pop. I haven't seen him in fifteen years."

Dictator-Parents are the tyrants of the parenting world. They see themselves as kings and their children as subjects. Or in some cases, they see themselves as masters and their children as property. They don't have a *relationship* with you, they *own* you. They control you with the threat of superior firepower. Dictator-Parents do not require your affection, only your fear, respect, and obedience. Dictator-Parents usually display a need to *diminish* their children with belittling comments.

When Melinda was nine years old, she ran home from school to report to her Dictator-Mother that she had won her class spelling bee. Having long sought her mother's elusive approval, she expected her mother to be pleased with the news. But when Melinda told Mom that she was the best speller in the class, Mom replied, "Must be a class full of dummies." Concludes Melinda today, "That's when I knew I would *never* gain her approval, no matter how hard I tried, no matter what I accomplished."

If there was a "Dictator-Parent's Handbook," it would contain such phrases as:

- "You'll never amount to anything!"
- "Or else!"
- "This is my house, and in my house you play by my rules!"
- "Because I told you to, that's why!"
- "You don't have to like it, you just have to do it!"
- "You'll never get it done your way!"
- "If you don't like it, there's the door!"

At some point in their lives, the children of a Dictator-Parent must choose among three options:

Rebellion. This is the choice Dirk made—the choice to fight his father and escape his domination. Some children will fight their Dictator-Parents to the death. In some cases, that battle may be colored by a sense of respect for Dad's towering and strong personality. In other cases, that battle may be colored with contempt and outright hated. Adult sons rebel by becoming as much the opposite of their Dictator-Parent as they can.

Adult daughters often rebel differently from sons, setting out in search of a man as different from Dad as possible—

perhaps a man who is weak and passive. The problem is that even though she despises her father's control and arrogance, she unconsciously admires his strength. Eventually she finds herself resenting her weak, passive partner. Having learned about gender roles from a Dictator-Father, her passive husband is not "man enough" by her standards.

Surrender. The child who attempts to rebel against the Dictator-Parent is often punished and punished until he finally surrenders. The child, unwilling to stand up to the parent directly, may carry on a passive "cold war" against the Dictator-Parent. For example, if the parent demands high grades in school, the child will perform at a mediocre or poor level. Ultimately, this behavior is only self-defeating, but at the time it seems like a way of *saving* the self from being squashed by the Dictator-Parent. A surrendered child is one who has a stormy relationship with the parent but who ultimately ends up under the parents' control and influence— perhaps growing up in the Dictator-Parent's mold, following in the parent's career footsteps, or even joining the Dictator-Parent in the family business.

Join. Some children figure out very early that most of the pain and pressure of a Dictator-Parent's style of parenting can be avoided by simply "getting with the program" and becoming a good soldier. You don't get yelled at and hit as much. You gain approval on the parent's own terms. Ultimately, the adult child "joiner" becomes a Dictator-Parent in her own family and a controlling terror to her own children. Dictator-Parents give the impression of towering, intimidating strength. Usually, however, there is a soft center of fear and vulnerability at the core of the Dictator's personality. He is scared to death of ever showing human weakness. Perhaps as a child, the Dictator was actually shunted aside and ignored and made a decision early in life: "Someday, people are going to notice me! They're going to pay attention to me! Someday, I'll be in control and anyone who opposes me will be sorry!"

He is, at his core, an insecure, frustrated, even frightened person.

How should you, as an adult child, respond to your Dictator-Parent? Here are some principles to help you:

Take a realistic look at your Dictator-Parent. Recognize the fact that this tower of power who has ruled your life for so long is truly and fundamentally a scared and insecure bully. He controlled you not only with fear but *out of* fear, and you don't have to be afraid anymore.

Recognize that you are an adult, an equal with your Dictator-Parent. You do not have to submit to your parent's intimidation and control any more.

In your present dealings with your Dictator-Parent, assert your independence firmly, strongly, and calmly. Show your parent that you are in control of your life *and your emotions* and that you will not yield that control to anyone, including your parent.

Be ready to resist old, familiar feelings. If your parent resorts to belittling and intimidation, you will feel old responses rising to the surface—fear, anger, defensiveness. If so, withdraw from your parent from a few moments, collect your thoughts and your feelings, pray, and then respond in a calm, controlled way.

Say, for example, "Since I was a child, you have frequently put me down, belittled me, and tried to frighten me. I don't know why you feel a need to make me feel small, but that is your problem, not mine. I know that I'm capable, that I'm strong, and that you can't control me anymore. And whenever you try to belittle me or control me, I'm going to turn around and walk away from you. I am ready to have a relationship with you whenever you are ready to respect me as an adult."

Focus on healing your own memories and emotions. Learn how to forgive and release bitterness (see chapter 12). If you are unable to let go of your resentment toward your Dictator-

Parent, your life will continue to be ruled and controlled by that parent even if she is dead. You cannot be your own person until you are free to live your life proactively. If you only live reactively—continually making choices out of anger and rebellion against a dictatorial parent—you are still in bondage to that parent.

Ben's Dictator-Father owned an appliance store. Since opening the store in the early 1960s, Ben's father had prospered. As Ben grew up, his entrepreneur-father groomed him to join him in the business, teaching Ben everything he had learned in "the school of hard knocks." He even handed Ben some hard knocks of his own. Ben never got an allowance; instead, he worked summers and after school in the store. Ben's father had no tolerance for mistakes from any of his employees, least of all from Ben. If Ben made a mistake, his father—the boss—screamed at and cursed him.

As Ben approached high school graduation, he told his father about his plans for college. "College!" his father snorted. "You don't need college to work in the family business! I never had a lick of college, and I did all right for myself. As soon as you graduate from high school, you'll come into the store. Within a year, if you produce enough sales, I'll make you floor manager."

"No, Dad," said Ben, "I'm going to college."

His father swore at him. "Well, don't think you're getting a nickel of my dough to waste on college! And don't expect me to hold a job for you when you get out of school!"

"I wouldn't work another day in your store for a million dollars!"

So Ben went to college. He paid for his education with scholarships, student loans, and money he earned flipping hundreds of burgers under the golden arches. He earned a bachelor's degree in business, then he went on to get an MBA. He came back to town and with the help of some investors and an Small Business Administration loan, he opened a discount electronics and appliance store down the street from his dad's store. Eighteen months later, he had put his dad out of business.

"My dad had made a lot of smart personal investments," Ben recalls, "so he was able to retire comfortably. But I broke the back of the business he spent a lifetime building. That was my dream—to break free of my dad's control by turning the tables on him. After he filed for corporate bankruptcy, I called him up. I guess I thought I was pretty cute. I offered him a job as floor manager in my store. He wasn't amused. He said, 'I spent years building that business from scratch. The day they put the sign over the door, I imagined one day handing the keys over to you. I never thought you would rather destroy it than own it. Ben, don't ever call or or come to this house again, do you understand?' That was the last time I ever spoke with him.

"I always thought it would taste sweet to beat that old tyrant at his own game. But I realize now I didn't beat him. I became just like him. And that doesn't taste sweet at all."

PARENTS WHO PROPHESIED

Mickey went into teaching because he loves young people and wants to be not only an instructor but a mentor. He modeled his life after the example of his own mentor, a high school teacher who had made a powerful impression on his life. During his first two years as a middle school teacher, Mickey felt he was really making a difference in the lives of his students. Some of them came to him with personal problems—family hassles, peer pressure, how to get help for drug or alcohol addiction—and he was gratified that he was able to point some of these kids in the right direction.

But when the school district fell on hard times and the budget axe fell, Mickey, young and untenured, was among the first teachers to be let go. He went on unemployment while job hunting, but his unemployment checks weren't enough to cover his mortgage and other expenses. When he found a job in another state, he put his house up for sale. Unfortunately, real estate prices had declined, and he was going to have to take a loss on the sale. Not having enough money to cover the deficiency, Mickey reluctantly went to his father for a loan.

"How much do you need son?" asked his father.

"Including closing costs, about eight thousand."

"That's a lot of money."

Mickey didn't respond. He knew that $8,000 was pocket change to his dad.

"Way back when you were in college," Mickey's father continued, "I told you this would happen. I told you to go into investment banking like I did. Or at least some area of financial management. But no, you wanted to be a teacher. You wanted to be a guiding light to the next generation. Didn't I tell you that if you became a teacher, you'd come to me begging for money one day? Well, you became what you wanted to be. Now you're stuck with it."

Parental prophecies can be a powerful and destructive force in our lives, controlling our destinies. For example, Liz's mother repeatedly told her that she was no good, that she couldn't be trusted, even though Liz never gave her mother any reason to make such a prophecy. Years later, when Liz was about thirty, that prophecy exploded like a land mine in her soul when she initiated an affair with a married man.

Brad's father always called him "The Klutz" because of the way he used to run into furniture and walls when he was just learning to walk. Somehow the name stuck throughout Brad's childhood, adolescence, and adulthood. His dad still thinks it's funny. But Brad has spent his entire life fulfilling what has become a very unfunny prophecy. He sees himself as clumsy, inept, and uncoordinated. He is a cautious driver, but because he is so nervous and lacking in confidence, he has had several accidents and has collected many tickets, including two for driving too slowly. He can't hold down a job for long because he gets nervous and makes mistakes in the presence of the boss. His father dubbed him "The Klutz," so a klutz he became.

We see the power of Parents Who Prophesied in the brief but profound story of Jabez in the Old Testament:

> Now Jabez was more honorable than his brothers, and his mother called his name Jabez [which literally means "he will cause pain"], saying, "Because I bore him in pain." And Jabez called on the God of Israel saying, "Oh, that You would bless me indeed, and enlarge my territory, that Your hand would be with me, and that You would keep me from evil, that I may not cause pain!" So God granted him what he requested.[1]

How would you like it if your mom named you Pain and told the whole neighborhood, "I named him Pain because that's what he is to me—a big pain!" Perhaps, in a sense, you *did* have such a parent. Parents name their children repeatedly throughout their lives, not just with names like "Joey" or "Suzie" but with names like "klutz" or "stupid" or "lazy" or even names that are unprintable.

The power to name a person is an awesome power. For example, the book of Genesis describes Adam as giving names to the animals—a symbol of Adam's God-given *authority* over creation.[2] When a parent names a child, that parent exercises enormous authority over that child. Names have meaning and weight and prophetic power.

The mother of Jabez named him, in effect, Pain-Bringer or Sorrow-Causer. She took her own pain and pinned it on her child, perhaps to get even with him for a harder than average labor. This prophecy set up an expectation and a horror in Jabez' soul: "I'm going to cause pain and sorrow! And I don't want to do that! How can I escape my fate?"

The child of a Parent Who Prophesied is lucky if the other parent will step in and protect him from that prophecy. That is what happened in Genesis 35. Rachel, the wife of Jacob, died shortly after giving birth to a son. Moments before she died, she named the baby boy Ben-Oni, meaning "son of my sorrow." But Jacob, the boy's father, stepped in and changed his name to Benjamin, meaning "son of my right hand."[3]

But what if there is no wise, strong parent in the picture to counter the prophecy of the unwise Parent Who Prophesied? That is the situation Jabez found himself in. His father may have been a wimp, or he may have been dead—but for whatever reason, no father came forward to stop him from being named Jabez, so the name stuck. But the good news in this story is that we do not have to accept the bad names and negative prophecies our parents impose on us. Jabez refused to accept his mother's prophecy, and he called upon God to help him escape those expectations.

Though he was born a Sorrow-Bringer, he lived and died a Blessing-Bringer. "Oh, that You would bless me," he prayed, "and that You would keep me from evil, that I may not cause pain!" And God granted his request. In effect, God granted Jabez a new prophecy and a new name and a new life. That is the way God works.

In the New Testament, we see the story of a man named Simon, which means "shifty one," a man of weak and unstable character. When Jesus encountered this man, he gave him a new name—Peter, which means "rock," suggesting solidity, stability, and strength. Simon didn't become a "rock" overnight. If you read his story in the Gospels, you see he vacillated between extremes of loyalty and defection, and he denied Jesus just moments before Jesus went to the cross. But after the resurrection, Jesus restored Peter, and Peter went on to be one of the principal founders of Christianity. He was transformed by the prophecy Jesus made in his life, and he went on to fulfill that new and positive prophecy in a big way.

Following are some suggested strategies for overcoming the hurtful prophecies of your parents:

Recognize the fact that you don't have to be defined by your parents' hurtful prophecies anymore. You are not responsible for the prophecies your parents dumped on you—but you are responsible to change and to become the person you want to be.

Pray. Ask God to give you a new name and a new future. Meditate in Scripture passages that affirm you and prophesy a positive future for you. Use the list of scriptural affirmations in chapter 6 as a starting point (see pages 108–109.)

Seek out friendships with people who will affirm you and build you up. A small group Bible study or a support group can be an excellent environment for repatterning your beliefs about yourself. Let the group do for you what your parents failed to do: give you a good name and a positive prophecy for your future.

Seek counseling from a professional counselor who can help you find the insight to understand how your life has been impacted by the prophecies of the past. Your image of yourself has been built up over years of influence from your parents, and it may take time for your old beliefs to be repatterned and restructured; but the healing will come if you commit yourself to the process.

Brent was a client of mine whose parents prophesied a dismal future for him. "You'll end up in a gutter with needle tracks up and down your veins," said his father, a prominent physician. "You'll bring shame on our whole family," predicted his mother, the socialite. Was Brent a drug addict? No. At that point, he had never even experimented with marijuana, much less the stuff that comes out of hypodermic syringes. Then why the dire prophecies?

"Because I wanted to be a musician," Brent explains. "It was all I wanted to do from the time I was about fourteen or so. We fought all the time about that—about my music and about a lot of stuff. They were horrified by my politics. They're somewhere to the right of Reagan, and I'm off to the left of Gorbachev. They didn't like the way I dressed or the friends I hung out with or the *Visualize Peace* bumper sticker on my car. So, naturally, they assumed I was destined to be a druggie. Every time the argument came up, out came the old predictions—the gutter, the needle tracks, shaming the family, the whole nine yards.

"I tried to treat it like a joke, you know? But it hurt. I mean, it really stung me, the fact that they really believed I would shoot up. I mean, I always took care of my body. My body is a temple, you know? I wouldn't have ever injected that stuff into my body."

Brent eventually got a music group together and started performing in clubs around the area. He was living on his own, sharing an apartment with another musician. One day, around Christmastime, Brent was visiting at his parents' home when the cycle started in again. "My folks and I got into this big argument thing," Brent recalls, "the same old song and dance, you'll end up in the gutter, and so on, and so forth. Well, I'd had it with that kind of stuff, so I lit out of there and slammed the door behind me. I went to hang out with my friends, and they were smoking and drinking and one of them was doing rock, you know, crack cocaine. I had always kept myself clean, you know, but that night I said, 'Let me have a hit of that stuff.'

"To this day, I can't figure out what I was thinking of. Was I trying to prove my parents were *wrong* about me by smoking crack? Or was I unconsciously trying to prove them *right*? I mean, either way, it's insane! I'll never understand it. I got hooked on crack after just one hit. It's powerful stuff. I spent a lot of time in rehab, and I still go to Narcotics Anonymous three times a week."

As Brent and I worked together on his issues, he began to understand that, even though he was an adult in his midtwenties, he still derived much of his identity from his parents. So I had Brent try a written exercise. I had him write down all the negative messages about himself that he had received from his parents. After he had written the negative messages down, he burned that list as a symbol of the fact that those messages no longer had control over him. Then I helped him set goals for himself. These were goals *he* wanted to achieve, not goals that his parents imposed on him or even goals that I, as his counselor, imposed on him. I suggested a category, such as a physical goal or a spiritual goal, and he stated what he wanted to achieve.

- Spiritual goal: "I will meet God every morning for fifteen minutes of prayer and Bible study."
- Mental/intellectual goal: "I will read one book a week for mental stimulation and relaxation."
- Physical goal: "I will run a mile every morning and limit myself to one Kit-Kat Bar a day." (Brent had been putting on weight since giving up cocaine, and Kit-Kats had become his new passion.)
- Occupational goal: "I will try to keep the band performing full-time." (Brent had been content to let club owners find his music group by word of mouth, which meant the group was often unemployed for as much as a month or two between gigs, and that left too much time on his hands. He decided to aggressively seek out contracts and keep performing year-round.)
- Relational goal: "I will continue to have a relationship with my parents, but I will lay down boundaries with them. I will tell them the kinds of messages they are not to give me anymore. If they violate those boundaries, I will reinforce to them the fact that I no longer receive those messages. I will help my parents understand that I am willing to have an adult relationship with them, but I will not accept their attempts to control me."

Brent turned this slate of goals into a covenant with himself which he reviewed, revised, and renewed every month. By setting his own goals for his life and focusing his energies on meeting those goals, he was able to finally free himself of the controlling predictions of his Parents Who Prophesied.

Whatever parenting style your parents employed, you are an adult now and you are free to make healthy choices and changes in your life. While your childhood has profoundly shaped you and affected you, the past does not control you.

"But you don't know my parents!" you may say. "You don't know the torment I've been through. I didn't just have an Unloving Parent or a Martyr Parent or a Parent Who Loved Too Much. I had a parent who tormented me and abused me and stole my childhood from me!" If that is your story, then turn the page. In the next chapter we will look at the most tragic and destructive cases of all: parents who physically or sexually abused their children.

6

Abusive and Seductive Parents

Ryan is twenty years old. Outwardly, he is a handsome young man with blond hair and blue eyes and an athletic build. In fact, he looks like a stereotypical California surfer. Inwardly, however, he is a mass of ugly scars. "When I was twelve," Ryan remembers, "I had this friend named Tom. The county took him away from his parents and put him in a foster home because they were beating up on him. I remember thinking, 'Luck-eee!' My folks didn't hit me, but I wished they did. If my dad had just given me one good beating, I could've turned them in and gotten out of there. All they did was 'verbal abuse.' I guess there's no law against that kind of abuse. But it hurts, man. It really hurts."

ABUSIVE PARENTS

Rita was in the emergency room of the hospital three times by the time she was seven years old, each time because (according to her parents) she had "fallen down the stairs." When Child Protective Services workers visited the house after the third incident, they discovered there were *no stairs* in the house! The last time Rita went to the hospital, her internal injuries were so bad she nearly died. Her right leg was shattered in several places and required three separate surgeries to correct the damage. Today she walks with a pronounced limp and still has metal pins in her right thigh.

"I can't remember anything of my first ten or eleven years," says Rita, now in her late twenties. "I don't remember my parents, my house, my school, my friends, or even the town I lived in. I have no memory of being abused, of being sad, of being happy, nothing. It's as if I didn't exist that whole time, and then I just sprang into existence in this foster home. I don't have memories. But I do have nightmares. I have lots of those."

Howard was six years old when his father flew into one of his frequent rages, picked Howard up, and hurled him headlong into a wall. The impact caused permanent brain and eye damage. Thereafter, Howard found it difficult to read and learn, was subject to occasional seizures, and frequently lost his balance. Howard's impairment caused his eyes to wander strangely, which gave him a unsettling appearance. He was a bright young man but severely limited by his impaired vision and appearance, so he found it hard to hold a job or to make friends. On Easter Sunday 1992, Howard got out of bed and started across the floor of his small apartment, heading for the kitchen. He never made it. He either had a seizure or lost his balance. In either case, he fell, cracked his head against the corner of a table, and died alone at the age of thirty-two. It is fair to say that Howard's death was a long-delayed but direct result of the injury his father had given him twenty-six years earlier.

There is a continuum of child abuse ranging from *verbal abuse* to *physical abuse* to *sexual abuse* (we will deal with sexual abuse in the next section, Seductive Parents). And while verbal abuse may not be a crime from a legal point of view, it is certainly one of the most destructive acts a parent can perpetrate against a child. Some verbal abusers are blatant and obscenely blunt:

- "I wish you were never born!"
- "Ugly, stupid brat!"
- "You're worthless!"

Merle was ten years old when his father went to prison. His mother never legally divorced his father, but she did take Merle and move him to another state. Merle never saw his father again, but he heard about his father continually: "You're just like that rotten, worthless father of yours! You look like him! You talk like him! You even *smell* like him!"

"She never really beat me," Merle recalls, "though she did slap my face sometimes. And she threatened to kill me all the time. You know how some parents say, 'Do that again and I'll whip you'? She'd say, "Do that again and I'll *kill* you!' And from the look in her eyes, I believed her."

And something else Merle believed throughout his childhood and on into adulthood: "I believed I was just as rotten and worthless as my old man. My mom had me convinced that a kid always turns out just like his father." Merle struggled with powerful suicidal urges for many years, and those feelings led him to seek counseling. He is now in a support group for abused adult children. He has made a lot of progress and understands that his feelings of worthlessness and his self-destructive urges were placed there by a sick, abusive mother, but he still has a long journey of healing ahead of him.

Other verbal abusers are more subtle than Merle's mother but no less harmful. They put their destructive messages in the form of insult humor, merciless teasing, sarcasm, and degrading nicknames. Jenny's mother thought it was funny to nickname her daughter "Buck" because of her protruding front teeth. And Gary's father would laugh while holding the screaming little boy over a stair railing three floors up or over a boiling pot of spaghetti. Then he'd berate Gary for being a "scared little chicken." Asked how they think their children feel about this kind of treatment, such abusers usually respond, "I was only teasing! The kid needs to learn to take a joke."

But children don't see this kind of parental behavior as joking or teasing—and it isn't. It's deliberately cruel, it's powerfully destructive, and it is the work of a sadistic, bullying personality. This kind of so-called "joking" and "teasing" would be harmful to adults, and is much more so to children. As the book of Proverbs says, "Like a madman who throws firebrands, arrows, and death, is the man who deceives his neighbor [or worse, his own child!], and says, 'I was only joking!'"[1]

Abusive relationships, whether verbal or physical, are the most powerful, stubborn, and intractable family patterns I ever see in my practice. Abusive families are very close families, and it is often very difficult to get an abused person to disengage from an abusive parent. There is usually a high degree of enmeshment; family members have little distance and few boundaries between one another. In abusive families, family members often seem to think each other's thoughts and assume they all have the same feelings. They see differences as betrayal. As a result, it is often extremely difficult for abused people to escape abusive situations.

The primary emotion most abused people have reported to me is *fear*—continual, grinding, gut-roiling fear. "I never knew what might set him off," is a common recollection. "I never knew when he might come into my room and start punching me and kicking me."

For many abusers, violence is a way of responding to marital stress, sexual frustration, job stress, or other specific "triggers" in life. But many other abusers don't need any external "trigger" to set them off. Like static electricity, an abuser's rage just seems to accumulate until it unexpectedly discharges in a lightning flash of fury. In that moment, an abuser seems to have no conscience, no sense of anyone's feelings but her own, not the least particle of restraint.

Some abusers are like something out of a horror movie. Their personalities are composed of 100 percent pure malevolence and hostility. They seem to lack even the most basic human components. They haven't a speck of compassion, or remorse, of tenderness. They live to hate.

Other abusers seem to alternate between violence and a starkly contrasting, enmeshed love. They send their children the most confusing, mixed messages imaginable. They will tell their children, "You're my whole life, I love you so much, you'll always be my baby," then they will lash out violently, inflicting unimaginable pain on the child. Moments later, they swing back to the other extreme, hugging the child and begging forgiveness.

Some abusers use the Bible as a justification for their violence. "Spare the rod and spoil the child" is a favorite cliché of these people. Yet the image we find in the Bible of what a parent is supposed to be is that of a gentle, loving, patient, nurturing person whose "rod" is a shepherd's staff, used to guide and protect, not to inflict suffering. The ultimate symbol of fatherhood in Scripture is God the Father, whom Jesus depicted in the parable of the Prodigal Son as one who doesn't beat and humiliate his erring children but rather receives and restores them. This is the Father of whom Psalm 23 says, "Your rod and Your staff, they *comfort* me."[2] In addition to being sadistic bullies of little children, religious abusers commit the additional crime of slandering God and poisoning the minds of children against the One who said, "Let the little children come to Me, and do not forbid them; for of such is the kingdom of God."[3]

The effects of verbal and physical abuse on a child are shattering and long-lasting. Adult children of Abusive Parents tend to:

- struggle with feelings of fear, guilt, anger, self-hate, suicidal urges, anxiety, tension, and depression.
- have enormous problems with relationships, such as marriage and relationships with their own children. Abused adult children often unconsciously sabotage their most important relationships, believing, "I don't deserve to be happy."
- repeat the abuse pattern and become abusers themselves. This cycle occurs because abused children tend to store up rage within themselves over the pain, humiliation, and terror they have suffered, but they haven't learned any healthy way to release those feelings. Instead, they practice what they have learned from their parents: if you feel enraged, take it out on someone smaller than you.
- identify with their abusive parents. Just as POWs sometimes come to identify with their captors and as Patty Hearst came to identify with her kidnappers, abused children look upon their towering, seemingly all-powerful parents and think, *'If I become like my abusive parent, no one can hurt me anymore. I will be the one doing the hurting!'*

As terrible as all these consequences are and as painful as they can be, there is good news: adult children of Abusive Parents can experience recovery and healing from the destructive legacy that has been inflicted on them. Here is a program of practical strategies you can apply to your own emotions, memories, behavior, and relationships:

Seek out counseling and a support group for survivors of abuse.

Clear your mind and your body of toxins. Before you can truly experience emotional and spiritual healing from the abuse of the past, you need to free yourself of any substance abuse if it is part of your life. To begin the task of gaining control over your addictions, begin with a medically supervised detoxification program (contact your local hospital or physician for a referral), followed by determined involvement in a Twelve Step program such as Alcoholics Anonymous or Narcotics Anonymous. *Daily attendance* at Twelve Step meetings is recommended in the first few months of your sobriety.

Accept the fact that you have choices and power. If there is an issue you are struggling with—standing up to your parents, saying no to them, confronting them—don't say, "I can't do that." Say, "I haven't done that *yet.*" Don't admit defeat or powerlessness. Commit yourself to growth and change.

Let yourself feel and express the anger inside you. You've blamed yourself long enough. Now it's time to fix the responsibility for your pain right where it belongs: with your abusive parents. They are the ones who hurt you, neglected you, humiliated you, made you feel unloved and unlovable. They wronged you, and you are not responsible for their abusive words and behavior.

Anger is an unpleasant emotion, and many of us shrink back from feeling it and expressing it. But you can't go under, over, or around anger on your way to emotional well-being. You must punch your way through it. Only then can you remove anger as an underlying issue in your life.

As long as you don't hurt yourself or anyone else with your anger, you should express it and get it out in the open. Express your anger in a letter to your parents. Express it verbally to a photograph of your parents. If you have feelings of violent anger, let something soft absorb your violent energy, such as a pillow, a sofa cushion, or a punching bag at the gym. Burn off angry energy with physical exercise, such as tennis, running, or handball. There is an added benefit to exercise: vigorous activity stimulates the production of endorphins, natural chemicals in the brain which enhance your sense of happiness and well-being.

Consider confronting your parents with the pain and abuse they have inflicted on you. Confrontation consists of:

- Telling your parents the painful events you remember from the past,
- Telling them how those events affected your childhood and your adult life,
- Telling them what aspects of your present relationship with them still cause you pain in the present, and
- Telling them what new rules and boundaries you intend to lay down for your future relationship with them.

Not everyone has the strength or even the need to confront their parents. Your parents may be too emotionally disturbed and destructive to confront. They may be dead or otherwise out of the picture. Don't feel you *have* to confront your parents in order to get on with your life; many survivors of abuse are able to gain strength and healing without a face to face confrontation with their parents. Consult your therapist or counselor before making the decision to confront. You should not go into a confrontational situation without specific strategies for what to say, how to respond when your parents counterattack, and how to keep from being sidetracked.

Make a daily habit of affirming and forgiving yourself (see the list of scriptural affirmations on pages 108 to 109).

Finally, *forgive* your abusive parents. Notice, I did not say you have to *reconcile* with them. In some cases, reconciliation with an abusive parent may be healthy, but understand two things: (1) A relationship with a parent who continues to be destructive, controlling, and abusive is almost certainly not in your best interests. (2) You do not have to reconcile in order to forgive. True forgiveness is a healthy process of removing hurtful people from the driver's seat of your life, so that you can live a healthy, inner-directed life, free of the control of other people. For a more complete discussion of forgiveness, see chapter 12.

The counselor sat quietly in the corner, saying nothing.

Aileen paced the floor. Though twin tracks of tears ran down her face, she was in control. Her mother sat on the sofa, her face buried in her hands, weeping ragged sobs. Her father sat next to her mother, fidgeting nervously.

"I've told you what you did to me, how it made me feel, and how your abuse has affected my adult life," said Aileen. "Now, I want to hear you have to say in response."

Aileen's father was twisted with barely controlled rage. His fists clenched and unclenched. "I can't believe I'm hearing this! All of these lies and accusations! No wonder you're seeing a shrink, Aileen. All this stuff you've been saying is crazy! You just cooked it all up out of your imagination!" He nudged his sobbing wife with his elbow. "Isn't that right, Louise?"

Aileen's mother looked up, her faced striped with mascara. She shrugged helplessly but said nothing.

"Oh, it all happened, Daddy," Aileen said adamantly. "I don't know if you are in denial or just lying, but it all happened. The beating with an electric cord on my bare bottom. The time you shoved my head in the toilet. The time you dragged me out of my bed and locked me outside all night. And a hundred other things I didn't even bother to bring up. Whether you choose to admit it or remember it, it all happened, Daddy, and you did it! And Mom, you let it happen! I begged you to stop him, and you just turned away!"

"Aileen," her mother pleaded, "what could I do? I couldn't have stopped him!"

"Louise!" her father snapped. "You shut your mouth! Doctor, I swear to you, that girl is lying! I never did anything to her but give her a good Christian spanking now and then when she needed it! If she was ever whipped, it was only because she had it coming! Trouble was, I wasn't tough enough on her! Look at her! We fed her, clothed her, gave her a good home, and this is how she repays us! Well, Doctor, aren't you going to say anything?"

"Aileen can speak for herself," replied the counselor.

"You bet I can," said Aileen. "Daddy, the beatings you gave me were not my fault. I wasn't bad. I didn't deserve to have my head shoved in a toilet. I'm not responsible for the any of the cruel things you did to me when I was little."

"I don't have to listen to this!" Her father ground the words between his teeth. He came up off the sofa. "Come on, Louise, we're getting outta here!"

"Fine," said Aileen. "Leave, if that's what you want to do, Daddy. I thought you were strong enough to hear the truth. The fact is, even after everything you've done, I'd still like to have a relationship with you. For one thing, I'd like to get to know you and understand you better. I'd like to understand what kinds of hurts you must have suffered that would make you beat up on a helpless little girl. I mean that sincerely. For another thing, I'd like for *you* to get to know *me* because I am one terrific person, and you'd really be depriving yourself if you missed the chance to find out who your daughter really is.

"But there's one thing you need to know, Daddy. You too, Mom. There will be no relationship between us until I hear you admit the truth of what happened and until you apologize for it—and I mean apologize specifically. For the beatings. For locking me out at night. For shoving me in the toilet. For everything. And there's more."

His face red with rage, Aileen's father advanced a step toward his daughter. Aileen flinched slightly but stood her ground. When her father saw that she was not going to be intimidated, he turned again to his weeping wife. "Get up, Louise," he said.

"After the apology, there are some new rules, Daddy," Aileen continued. "I'm through accepting your abuse. From now on, no more name-calling or yelling at me. No more ridicule. No more calling me crazy or stupid. And if you can't abide by my rules, then you'd better just stay out of my life."

Aileen's father grabbed his wife by the hand and pulled her

off the sofa and out of the office. His muttering and cursing could be heard all the way to the elevator.

To date, Aileen has received no apology or any other contact from her parents. Perhaps she never will. If Aileen's parents do not respond favorably to her confrontation, then Aileen has lost very little. They never had a true relationship before the confrontation, and the confrontation was really the only chance they had of finally building a *real* relationship. Either way, whether her parents come around or not, Aileen feels she has gained a lot. "I found out I had a lot more strength and courage than I thought," she says today. "It was tough, but not as tough as I thought it would be. And now I know that, regardless of the past, I'm okay."

SEDUCTIVE PARENTS

Francie is a kindergarten teacher in her mid-twenties. She has an engagement ring on her finger and a troubled expression on her face. She is a virgin. Her pending marriage has raised anxieties in her mind about sex. "The whole idea of opening myself up to a man just petrifies me," she says. "Just in the past few weeks, I've remembered a lot of things I hadn't thought of in years, and I think these memories are flooding back because I'm about to be married."

What sort of memories?

"Memories of my father watching me. He'd come into my bedroom without knocking when I was getting dressed. He'd come into the bathroom when I was taking a shower. I'd lock the door, but he knew how to spring the latch. He never touched me, but he was always looking at me, always telling me I had a beautiful body. It was . . . creepy."

Bob was eight years old when he was first seduced by his mother. This incestuous pattern continued until Bob's mother was killed in a traffic accident when he was sixteen. "First, she did it to me, then she had me do it to her," he recalls in a trembling voice. "She'd say, 'This is something people do when they love each other.' That made it sound like it was okay. Then she'd also say, 'If you tell anyone what we did, your father will hate you. He might even kill you. What we did was very private, and no one can ever know.' I never told anyone about this until I went into counseling. Even after my mother died, I never told anyone. I've never even told my wife. How can you tell anyone that your own mother did *that* to you?"

Eve was fifteen when the police removed her from her home and took her father into custody. Eve had confided in her friend Darcy that her father had been having sex with her since she was nine years old. Darcy told a school counselor, and the school counselor called the authorities.

I met with Eve at the foster home where she was temporarily placed by Child Protective Services. "Daddy was right," she said between big, wracking sobs. "He said that if I ever told anyone, the police would take him to jail and our family would never be together again, and he was right. I should have kept my big mouth shut. This is all my fault."

Later that same day, Eve's mother was in my office. She too thought it was all Eve's fault. "My husband is a good man, a deacon in the church!" she fumed as she paced around the room. "If he had ever done such an awful thing to Eve, I would know, wouldn't I? Eve's a little liar! She could never be trusted! And her friend, what's her name? Darcy! I'm sure Darcy put Eve up to this! You know all the terrible things kids see on TV and in the movies these days! All those stories about sex and the things that go on in sick families! Darcy and Eve got to talking and they just made this whole thing up! That's the only explanation! I mean, something like this couldn't go on under my roof for—how many years did she say? six? seven years?—without me knowing about it!"

Sexual abuse is without question one of the cruelest acts a parent can perpetrate against a child. The seduction and sexual exploitation of a child strikes at the most fundamental possession any child has: childlike innocent trust. In this behavior, the one who should be the child's natural protector becomes a predator.

Because the legal definition of incest tends to be very narrowly defined in most states, many people are confused as to just what constitutes the sexual abuse of a child by a parent. Some people presume that to be considered incest or sexual abuse, the activity must include sexual penetration. Actually, a child can be sexually abused without even being touched. Here are some of the behaviors which clearly come under the heading of sexual abuse and which are very damaging to the emotional and psychological well-being of a child:

- Exposing oneself or committing sexual acts (including masturbation) in front of a child
- Photographing or videotaping a child in sexually suggestive poses
- Touching or fondling a child for the sake of one's own sexual arousal and gratification
- Inducing a child to masturbate in order to produce sexual arousal or gratification in oneself
- Invading a child's sexual privacy by watching the child dress or bathe, making seductive or sexually suggestive comments or jokes, complimenting the child in a sexual way, exposing the child to pornographic material, or talking to the child about one's own sexual behavior
- Sexual intercourse with a child (anal, oral, or vaginal)

It may be that some of these acts were committed against you in your childhood, and though you find the memories of those acts disturbing and painful, you never thought of them before as *abuse*. Perhaps these acts were done to you not by a blood relative but by a stepparent or someone else who was under the family's roof. Even so, the psychological ramifications are usually the same in such cases as in *incest* (which is technically defined as sexual relations between closely related people). A stepparent, an uncle, or any other visiting or live-in adult tends to be viewed and trusted by the child on a level approaching that of a biological parent. Plus there is the psychological harm that comes when that abusive person bullies the child into silence with such threats as "If you tell, I'll kill you," or "Nobody will believe you. They'll say you're crazy or bad or you made it all up."

Some of the effects an incestuous relationship can produce in a child or an adult child are:

Intense feelings of shame, worthlessness, and guilt. Incest survivors often describe themselves as feeling "dirty." They frequently accept the blame for what was done to them.

Intense fusion with the abusive parents. Ironically, even though abusive parents are the source of the adult child's pain and emotional dysfunction, the incest survivor frequently seeks support and consolation from those same abusive parents. The incest survivor often is as involved as the parents in denying the problem and protecting the family from the painful truth. The irony of abuse—whether physical, verbal, or sexual—is that abusive families are very close families.

Masking of emotions, particularly painful emotions. Incest survivors often say, "I'm okay," when they are not. They often have a difficult time handling and expressing anger.

Feeling robbed of a normal childhood. "I never had a chance to just be a kid," is a common expression. Incest survivors often feel conspicuously abnormal and out of place in the world.

An inability to set boundaries or say "no" to others. Incest survivors tend to ignore their own needs and well-being in order to meet the needs or demands of others. They believe that other people are important and that they themselves are unimportant.

Vulnerability to being exploited and abused by others. Incest survivors tend to gravitate toward abusive, exploitative people. They often symbolically continue the childhood struggle with their abusive parent through adult relationships with other people, trying to get these other abusive people to change or to love them.

An inability to trust other people. Incest survivors tend to feel it is common to be betrayed and exploited in life, and this belief makes them wary in relationships.

An inability to enjoy sex and sensuality. Some incest survivors are sexually inhibited. Others may enjoy sex but feel guilty and dirty after sex, even perfectly healthy sex within marriage. The sex act has been, in effect, spoiled and sullied for the incest survivor because he always associates sex with the abuse he experienced in childhood.

An inability to enjoy life. "I don't deserve to be happy," is a common expression of incest survivors.

You may be suffering from many of these consequences of childhood sexual abuse. But there is hope, and there is help available. You can experience healing from the abuse of the past. Here are some workable strategies you can apply in your own life:

Understand that what happened to you was not your fault. You do not share any of the blame or responsibility for being abused as a child.

It is not uncommon for adult children of Seductive Parents to say, "But I *am* responsible! I actually *enjoyed* it! I experienced sexual pleasure from the experience! How can you say I'm not to blame?" But the fact remains that the perpetrator of the abuse, not you, must shoulder *all* the responsibility. Your body was designed to respond to sexual stimulation, and the abuser merely took advantage of that fact for his own gratification. You didn't do anything wrong. You were used and exploited by another person, and you need to stop accepting any portion of the blame, which belongs completely with the abuser. The person who abused you was an adult, and you were a child. An adult is responsible for controlling his own behavior in the presence of children, no matter what. Period. End of story.

Recognize that if you were sexually violated by one parent, it will be quite natural to feel betrayed by both parents. If, for example, you are a daughter who has been sexually abused by your father, you almost certainly either suspect or know that your mother was a silent accomplice to your father's abuse. Of course, it's possible that Mom really didn't know. In many cases where the abuse continued over a long time, Mom *chose* not to know; she lived in denial, hoping the problem would go away and the family would stay together and everything would turn out all right. Sometimes the mother clearly and unambiguously knows—she sees the act of abuse in progress or the child tells her about the abuse—and she does nothing about it. When that happens, the child feels outrageously betrayed by both parents. Even if you were abused by only one parent, you will probably need to deal with anger and hurt toward both parents.

Make a daily habit of affirming and forgiving yourself (see the list of scriptural affirmations on pages 108 to 109).

Consider confronting your parents with the pain and abuse they have inflicted on you. For a more detailed explanation of what confrontation entails, see the section on confronting Abusive Parents, pages 91 to 101.

Seek out counseling and a support group for survivors of sexual abuse. Don't suffer alone. Don't suffer any longer than you have to. Don't try to attempt your therapy alone, by reading this or any other book. This book is not intended as a substitute for therapy. Professional help and peer support are essential resources for those who have been sexually abused as children. And the good news is that the very issues you are facing can almost always be resolved, positively and effectively, with the help of a professional counselor. It is an act of courage and a sign of growing strength and emotional health to deal with your abuse.

You may be thinking, "What's wrong with me? My parents and other family members are going on with their lives as if nothing happened, yet I'm miserable all the time! I must be really sick!" In fact, quite the opposite is true.

Even though the person who was abused displays all the outward symptoms of dysfunction (depression, weeping, anger, self-destructive urges), she is usually the *healthiest* person in that whole family system. The others in the family—those who committed the abuse and those who looked the other way while the abuse was going on—continue to deny reality and defend themselves and each other. They are still sick, but you are already starting to get well. You may be feeling pain, you may be crying all the time, you may be experiencing horrible memories and feelings, *but all of these symptoms are a sign that you are getting better and stronger!* Your mind and emotions are telling you that you have finally gained the strength to deal with the past and flush it out of your life for good.

So take that courageous step. Deal with past so you can live in the present and face the future.

DEALING WITH WHATEVER KIND
OF PARENT YOU HAD

We have examined several different kinds of parents in this and the previous chapter. Whatever kind of parent you had, there are steps you can take to reverse the harmful effects of the way you were parented in the past. Here are some general strategies for dealing with the emotional debris left over from your childhood:

Practice giving grace to yourself. Whenever you make a mistake, forgive yourself.

Try this mental exercise: What are some of the things about yourself which you feel are absolutely awful? What are the secrets about yourself which make you feel, "No one would love me if they knew . . ."? Imagine that those are not *your* secrets and flaws but the secrets and flaws of someone you respect. Now, how do you feel about that person? Do you want to hate that person, or do you think, "No big deal"? Chances are, the imperfections that you hate in yourself are imperfections you would easily tolerate and forgive in someone else. So forgive yourself, just as you would forgive those flaws in another person.

Make self-affirmation a daily discipline. Combine it with your daily prayer and Bible reading. Put up cards on your mirror or in your Bible or on the dashboard of your car which say, "God made me, God loves me, God forgives me." Or "I am my own person, making my own way." Or "I accept myself exactly as I am." Or "The past is past. I live in the present."

Meditate on Scripture passages which affirm your God-given self-worth. In his book *Please Let Me Know You, God,* Dr. Larry Stephens includes a valuable list of affirming statements for Christians, taken from Scripture. I have abridged and adapted that list as follows:

- I am loved with an everlasting love (Jer. 31:3).
- I am set free (John 8:31–33).
- I have abundant life (John 10:10).
- I am a saint (Rom. 1:7).
- I am free of shame and condemnation (Rom. 8:1).
- I am a joint heir with Christ (Rom. 8:17).
- I am being changed and conformed to the image of Christ (Rom. 8:28–29, Phil. 1:6).
- I am more than a conqueror through Christ (Rom. 8:37).
- I am a temple of the Holy Spirit (1 Cor. 6:19).
- I am a new creation (2 Cor. 5:17).
- I am holy and without blame before God (Eph. 1:4).
- I am accepted in Christ (Eph. 1:6).
- I am forgiven; all my sins are washed away (Eph. 1:7).

- I am sealed by the Holy Spirit (Eph. 1:13).
- I am God's workmanship (Eph. 2:10).
- I am strong in the Lord (Eph. 6:10).
- I have the peace of God, which surpasses understanding (Phil. 4:7).
- I can do all things through Christ (Phil. 4:13).
- I am complete in Christ (Col. 2:10).
- I am beloved and chosen by God (Col. 3:12; 1 Thess. 1:4).
- I have been called by God (2 Tim. 1:9).
- I am God's forever-child (1 Peter 1:23).
- I am healed by the wounds of Christ (1 Peter 2:24).
- I am victorious (Rev. 21:7).[4]

Meditate on the Serenity Prayer of Reinhold Neibuhr: "God grant me the serenity to accept the things I cannot change, the courage to change the things I can, and the wisdom to know the difference."

Cultivate friendships with people who affirm you and build you up. Join a small group Bible study or a support group (such as a group for adult children of dysfunctional families).

At the same time you are working on your own emotional issues and rebuilding your confidence and self-esteem, you will also want to consciously, deliberately shape the boundaries of your relationship with your parents, both for your welfare and theirs. Here are some general principles and specific insights to help you sculpt a healthy relationship with the people who raised you:

Don't expect your parents to change. They certainly won't change overnight, and they may not ever change, so accept them as they are. Don't base your happiness and security on whether or not your parents "see the light." You can still take charge of your life and be your own person. You can choose to change and grow even if your parents choose not to.

Try to understand what makes your parents behave the way they do—not to excuse them but so that you can be better equipped to deal with them. Find out as much as you can about your parent's childhood, plus any adult experiences that may have dramatically affected his personality. You may find that underneath that difficult exterior is a hidden person who is very fearful or very needy. By understanding those fears and needs, you may be able to find creative, healing ways to reduce the antagonism between you and your parent.

If you find yourself being repeatedly drawn into conflict or into being manipulated by your parents, focus on strategies for staying in control of yourself. Avoid defensiveness. Avoid responding in kind when your parents sulk, manipulate you, or attack you. Respond in a nondefensive manner:

- "You are entitled to your opinion, but I am also entitled to mine."
- "I understand that you don't approve of my choices, but they are *my* choices."
- "I can see you're upset. Why don't we talk about this later, when we can discuss it calmly."
- "I can see this is hard for you."
- "Let me think about what you've said."
- "I've heard you out, now I would like you to hear what I have to say."
- "Screaming at me isn't going to accomplish anything."
- "I understand you are feeling hurt and angry, but that's not my problem. That's something you need to solve yourself."
- "Let's try to keep this conversation on a productive level."

Understand that when you respond this way, your parents will probably escalate their pressure and attacks on you. They are accustomed to controlling your behavior, and when they discover they no longer control you, they may become enraged and frustrated. Don't let them pull you back into un-healthy and unproductive behavior patterns.

Consider writing a letter to your parents. In the letter, hon-estly lay out your feelings and the specific things they have done which have hurt you. You may or may not decide to ac-tually mail the letter. (It would be wise to get objective coun-sel from a trusted friend or therapist before taking such a step.) Just getting your feelings out can often be a helpful way to release bitterness and resentment.

Consider confronting your parent face to face. If you don't feel you can do this by yourself, involve a counselor in the process, both to offer insight and to give you moral support so that you can say what needs to be said. Don't expect your parent to respond positively or to change her behavior. Don't even expect your parent to hear what you are saying. Be pre-pared for anger, manipulation, crying—all the behavior you have experienced before, only magnified. Before you attempt such a confrontation, map out a strategy with your counselor: "If she says X, I should respond with Y." Remember that this situation is like a chess game, and you need to have your moves and countermoves planned in advance.

When interacting with your parent, practice effective com-municating. Say exactly what you mean, avoiding double messages or sarcasm. Express your own needs and your own feelings. If your parent denies, manipulates, or tries to con-trol your message ("Don't be silly, son. Of course you like it when I send you money; everybody likes money"), restate your message in firm, clear terms ("No, Dad, I am absolutely serious about this, and I want you to listen to me very closely: do not send me any more money"). Own your own feelings by using "I" statements: "I get frustrated when you do that," not "You make me mad when you do that."

If you experience guilt, anxiety, or agitation over drawing boundary lines in your relationship with your parents, try to determine the source of those feelings. They could spring from the childhood conditioning you received. You may be thinking, *If I seek my own emotional health, my own relation-ships, and my own goals, then I'm betraying my parents!* Or those feelings could spring from a scared and childlike part of you that, at some unconscious level, still clings to your parents as the godlike shapers of your personality, your goals, and your behavior. Remember that you are a fully liberated, separate, equal adult. You don't need parents defining and shaping your life any more. In fact, you have a responsibility to shape your own life in accordance with your own goals and with God's will.

Every child was born with a need for these ingredients for a healthy and happy life:

- A childhood of innocent joys, free of the pressures, trials, and responsibilities of adulthood.
- A sense of control, accomplishment, and healthy self-direction in life.
- Unconditional acceptance and validation of who he truly is.
- Respect for his own feelings and thoughts.

Unfortunately, not every child receives these basic minimum requirements for a healthy, happy life. Perhaps you are one of the ones who didn't. But that doesn't mean you are doomed to an unhappy, unhealthy existence for the rest of your life. It just means you have some work to do.

I've seen hundreds of people begin that work at the very point where you are now. I've seen them courageously un-cover the secrets and uncork the emotions and unlock the painful memories. I've seen the tears and heard the pain—but I've also witnessed the moments when joy and understanding and light broke through, when discoveries were made, when healing took place.

If there is any hesitation in your mind right now, I encourage you to listen to the urgency in your heart. Take the first step toward healing. Get the help you need. Do it *now*.

In the next chapter, we will explore practical strategies for setting healthy boundaries in the relationship with our parents.

7

Setting Boundaries

"My husband is a big, overgrown adolescent," Jolene complained, sitting in my counseling office. "He's twenty-seven going on twelve. He's never had to grow up and take responsibility. He won't stay in one job more than six months. He just says, 'I'm bored with this job!' and he quits, just like that! We get bills, past due notices, cutoff notices, and he just ignores them! Before we got married, I had good credit, my own car, and eight thousand dollars in the bank. Now the house has two mortgages, we're maxed out on credit cards, and every time the phone rings it's a bill collector! I want Tony to grow up and start taking responsibility."

I had a feeling as I listened to Jolene that these problems, as serious as they were—Tony's lack of motivation, his inattention to pressing financial problems, his apparent immaturity—were just the symptoms of a deeper problem. The more Jolene described her unhappy life with Tony, the more one question continued to gnaw at me: How in the world did these two people ever manage to marry each other? It's true that opposites attract, but there was hardly *anything* Tony and Jolene had in common!

Jolene was a career woman from a wealthy family. Her husband Tony was from a family of poor immigrants. By any standard you might apply—ethnic background, socio-economic status, religion, career goals, values, education, or tastes in music, entertainment, and recreation—Tony and Jolene were a study in contrasts. They seemed to come from different planets.

I could only find one area of common ground: neither of them had any boundaries. Jolene's complaints centered around the way Tony's parents continually interfered with their private life. Tony's mother would call and say, "Jolene, dear, I'll be over at 9 A.M. on Saturday, so if any of Tony's clothes need mending, have them ready by then, okay?" She told Jolene what kinds of foods to fix for Tony, where they should go on vacation, and even when they should start a family.

Tony's brothers and sisters were just as intrusive. When visiting, they thought nothing of going into Tony and Jolene's bedroom, pawing through their closet, and simply borrowing clothes without even asking. And that wasn't all they borrowed. One time Jolene came home to find the car missing, the kitchen window jimmied open, and a note on the kitchen table, written by one of Tony's brothers. It read: *Jolene, I took the extra keys out of your jewelry box. Knew you wouldn't mind. I'll have the car back tomorrow morning.*

Jolene seethed with rage as she spilled her story in my office. "When I married Tony," she said bitterly, "I never thought I'd be marrying his whole obnoxious family! I might as well have stayed a child and never left home for all the privacy I have with Tony."

A clue! I connected her last comment with something she had said earlier about her own upbringing. She had told me of the enormous difficulty she had separating from her own family. Her mother still held tremendous influence over her. On her frequent visits, Jolene's mother never hesitated to ask invasive questions about her sex life, to rearrange her furniture and decor, or to run a finger over the piano top, checking for dust.

"Jolene, I'm curious," I said at last. "Why did you ever marry a guy like Tony?"

"What do you mean?"

"Well, what was it that attracted you to him?"

She looked at the floor and was silent for a long time. Then she said, "I was attracted to him because he was different."

"Different from what?"

"Different from me. Different from my background. I think I was attracted to him because my parents didn't approve of him."

"In other words," I said, "you might say that Tony helped you feel a sense of separation and independence from your parents. He symbolized freedom from your parents and your upbringing."

A light went on in her eyes. "You know, I never thought of it that way, but I guess you're right. And the crazy thing is—I'm still not free. I feel more trapped than ever."

Jolene had made a profound discovery about her marriage: neither she nor Tony had ever really separated from their parents and families. They had never truly left home. They had no boundaries around their relationship, and their own family was not yet established.

THE WELL-BOUNDED COUPLE

Healthy families are well-bounded families. Healthy couples are composed of two people who have left their respective families and have established clear physical and emotional boundaries between themselves and their childhood families—and between themselves and the rest of the world.

The successful separation of a person from his childhood family is a complicated, two-step maneuver. In step one, the parents release their emotional claims on the child. In step two, the child steps out of the grasp of the parent.

First, let's look at step one. This step is the goal of all good parenting: to raise a child to be a happy, mature, responsible adult and to release that child into the world. Throughout the child's growing years, a nurturing parent will constantly find ways to challenge the child and help her to discover and develop new strengths and abilities. The parent affirms achievements and guides the child in ways that are appropriate for each stage of development. The parent also maintains an appropriate—and gradually diminishing—level of control for each stage of a child's emotional and intellectual maturity until at young adulthood all control is finally relinquished.

But some parents fail to relinquish control. The parent who clings to the child in a smothering way is usually insecure and tends to project his own feelings of inadequacy on the child. This makes it harder for the adult child to take responsibility for himself or herself in an appropriate way. Both Tony and Jolene had parents who were insecure, repressive, and overbearing. The intrusiveness of Tony and Jolene's parents stunted their ability to firmly establish their own relationship.

Step two of this two-step maneuver is that the child must step out of the grasp of the parent. When two people marry, each partner must separate effectively from his or her family in order to establish a healthy boundary around the relationship. If one or both partners remains enmeshed with the childhood family, then that couple will not have effective boundaries, and the stage will be set for repeated conflict and intrusions from the childhood families.

The boundary that a healthy couple builds around the marriage relationship serves a double purpose. It keeps some things out while keeping other things in. A well-bounded couple recognizes that certain people, certain actions, certain words are off-limits to outsiders.

When Ted allows his best friend Jack to make passes at his wife, he has clearly failed to establish a healthy boundary around his marriage relationship.

When Eloise shares some of the sexual intimacies between

herself and her husband with her oldest daughter, she has crossed the boundary.

When Kate acts disloyally toward her husband, revealing his most embarrassing secrets and making him the butt of jokes in front of family and friends, she is destroying the protective boundary around their marriage relationship.

A boundary establishes a line of safety and security between the couple and the surrounding world. Boundaries enable us to say, "This is who *I* am. This is who *we* are. This is how *I* should act. This is how *we* should act." Such boundaries are absolutely crucial to the process of forming and maintaining a healthy, intact relationship.

THE WELL-BOUNDED INDIVIDUAL

The ability to make a healthy separation from our childhood families is directly related to our ability to form a strong, secure individual identity. When we are able to leave our childhood family with our parents' blessing and approval, we are able to say, "I am confident in who I am. I have a good sense of my own strengths, resources, abilities, and limitations. I'm willing to take responsibility for myself. My parents, too, have proved their faith in me and have endorsed my individuality by letting me go."

There's a beautiful paradox in the process of separating from our childhood family and becoming a well-bounded individual: it is our separateness that allows us to fully enter into a close and permanent bond with another person in a marriage relationship. The paradoxical (and thus profound) truth of a healthy marriage is that two separate, well-defined people can enter into a relationship so intimate that it borders on emotional fusion, yet each person maintains his or her own uniqueness and individuality.

Just as each marriage needs a boundary around it, so each partner within the marriage also needs a boundary around himself or herself, a sense of personal individuality and identity. Each must be able to say to the other, "This is who I am as opposed to you. These are *my* thoughts, *my* feelings, *my* desires, *my* goals." In every healthy couple, there are boundaries between each partner, plus a boundary around the marital relationship, and that includes clear boundaries between the marriage partners and their respective parents.

It is equally important for single people to have clear boundaries between themselves and their parents. Married or single, we all need to have our own goals, our own convictions, our own dreams, our own sense of direction in life. We are not truly adults until we have hammered out, tested, and refined our own values and ideals in the laboratory of life.

In order to have healthy relationships and a healthy view of ourselves, we need to clearly define these boundaries:

- **Emotional Boundaries**
- **Control Boundaries**
- **Time Boundaries**
- **Financial Boundaries**

Let's examine each of these areas in turn.

EMOTIONAL BOUNDARIES

Renee and her father were always the best of buddies. To Renee, her father wasn't "Dad." She called him Tom. "I never knew my mother," she recalls. "Tom hardly ever talked about her, even when I asked. He just told me she 'skipped out' on us when I was a year old. That's all I know."

Looking back, Renee realizes that her father was always poor though she never felt deprived in any way. "Tom moved around a lot," says Renee. "I had lived in at least thirty states by the time I was twenty. Tom did odd jobs. He still gets by that way, doing fix-it work and handyman jobs, doing yardwork, trimming palm trees, taking care of swimming pools, you name it.

"We always lived in dinky apartments or hotel rooms, and sometimes we slept in the same bed. He never did anything bad to me. You know, nothing sexual. We were just real close. Whenever he had some money in his pocket, he would buy me things. Dresses or dolls or whatever I wanted. And he took me to museums and movies and concerts and the zoo— I bet I've seen all the best zoos from San Diego to the Bronx. Because of the kind of work he did, his hours were very flexible, so he'd work while I was in school, and then after school we spent all our time together. He called me his pal.

"Tom got married once when we were living in Colorado. It didn't last long. I was ten years old at the time, and I sabotaged it. But they would have broken up sooner or later without my help. It was more her idea than Tom's.

"We had a great life until I got old enough to date. He wouldn't let me date at all until I was seventeen. We had a lot of fights about that. I wanted some freedom, some room to be myself, and Tom felt like I was rejecting him. A couple times, Tom saw that I was really getting interested in some boy so, 'Oops! Time to move on!' And we'd pull up stakes and move to another state.

"Finally, I got old enough so that he couldn't pull that on me. He'd say, 'Time to move on,' and I'd say, 'Fine, Tom. See ya. Don't forget to write.' He tried to call my bluff a few times, but when he figured out that I was staying put, so did he. That's pretty much where things have been for the last ten years. I've gotten involved with a dozen or more different men over the past ten years, and although I thought each one was Prince Charming for a while, they all turned out to be losers. I sure can pick 'em. And every time one of those guys would break my heart, I'd run back to Tom and cry my eyes out, and we'd go back to sharing an apartment and doing everything together until the next heartbreaker would come along.

"I'm thirty-odd years old now," Renee concludes, "and

Tom still wants me to stay with him. I think I should be building a life of my own by now, and I also think Tom is getting in the way of that, but I don't know what to do. I don't want to hurt Tom, but I really need a life of my own."

Renee has illustrated one of the key reasons why emotional enmeshment is so hard to escape: it is a pattern that was formed in the earliest years of childhood. These unhealthy patterns of early enmeshment are inevitably perpetuated in the present, *unless we can break the old cycles and set ourselves free of the patterns that bind us.*

How well-defined are the emotional boundaries between you and your parents? To find out, take the brief Emotional Boundaries Quiz, below:

(Check true or false.)

T ____ F ____ I often feel guilty about spending too little time with my parent or parents.

T ____ F ____ When I see or sense that my parents are hurting, I feel responsible and feel I need to do something about it.

T ____ F ____ My parent or parents rely on me as a source of happiness and emotional support.

T ____ F ____ My parent or parents discouraged me from moving away from home.

T ____ F ____ My parent or parents frequently shared intimate confidences and secrets with me.

T ____ F ____ I feel closer to one parent than the other.

T ____ F ____ I have been my parent's best friend.

T ___ F ___ I often share information with my parents
(about my social life, finances, career
decisions, and so forth) that is really
none of their business.

T ___ F ___ One of my parents preferred my company to
that of his or her spouse.

T ___ F ___ One of my parents told me or conveyed to me
that I was his or her favorite or "special"
child.

T ___ F ___ My parent or parents did not want me to date
or marry.

T ___ F ___ One of my parents seemed overly interested
in my sexuality and my body.

T ___ F ___ I often find myself explaining or defending my
parents to other people.

If you scored four or more "True" answers on this quiz, then there is a strong likelihood that you have a problem with emotional enmeshment with your parents and need to define clearer boundaries with your parents in the emotional dimension of your relationship.

Here are seven keys to defining clearer emotional boundaries in your relationship with your parents:

1. *Accept your parents as they are.* Accept the past and everything your parents have done. You can't change the past, so acknowledge it as a fact and get on with your life. Accept the way your parents act and feel; don't feel you are responsible for changing their behavior or their feelings. Accepting your parents, along with their past and present feelings and behavior, does not mean you have to like them or the way they

act. It simply means that you make a healthy decision *not* to take on the responsibility for your parents' feelings and behavior. An emotionally enmeshed person continually feels responsible and guilty toward his parents, while an emotionally healthy person places a boundary line of acceptance in this area of the relationship.

2. *Examine your reasons for continuing in an emotionally enmeshed relationship with your parents.* Recognize that you have some responsibility for the lack of emotional boundaries. Acknowledge that, in many of the painful or confusing dealings you have with your parents, you have actually *allowed* or *invited* the intrusion.

Perhaps you spend too much time with your parents because you are trying to atone for some act you committed against them many years ago. Perhaps because of feelings of guilt, you sometimes find yourself confiding or admitting things to your parents that are none of their business. Perhaps you find yourself sacrificing your own needs because you feel you owe some debt to your parents or you feel responsible for their happiness. *If so, then you are voluntarily giving up your own boundaries and inviting your parents to intrude on your life because of your own emotional enmeshment.*

These feelings and attitudes of guilt, debt, and responsibility toward parents may be very deeply submerged within you and hard to get in touch with. On the surface, you may not realize the emotional motivations that are driving your enmeshed behavior. To you, the problem may be a fuzzy sense of powerlessness: "I don't know how to draw emotional boundaries. I feel trapped, I'm completely overwhelmed by them—almost as if I have no will of my own. My parents need me. It would destroy them if I pulled back from them. There's nothing I can do."

There *is* something you can do, but you can't see it now. You need some help in gaining an understanding of the inner forces which keep you emotionally bonded to your parents. A professional counselor can help you turn your fuzzy sense of powerlessness into insights and practical strategies for defining clear emotional boundaries with your parents.

3. *Seek to order your loyalties and emotional attachments according to God's plan.* Biblically, we are to love God first and then love others and ourselves according to a hierarchy of priorities. That hierarchy looks like this:

God	**Highest priorities**
Spouse	
Children	
Family of Origin (Parents)	↑
Fellow Christians	
Neighbors	**Lowest priorities**

Pray for wisdom, insight, and strength to put your relationship with your parents in its proper place in that hierarchy of loyalties. Your relationship with your parents should not more important than your relationship with God, nor be more important than your marriage relationship and your own needs, nor more important than your relationship with your own children. If it is, then seek God's help and strength in drawing clearer boundaries in that relationship.

4. *Plan a strategy for talking with your parent about emotional boundaries.* Put your wishes in positive rather than negative terms. Instead of saying, "I need to pull back from you," say, "I want to improve our relationship. I think it would be healthy for us both to find more time for our own goals and our own interests. You and I have taken too much responsibility for each other's happiness and well-being, and I would like to see us have a more balanced relationship. I want us to be completely open with each other about our needs and desires. If you need more time to pursue your own interests, I want you to feel free to come right out and say so.

And if I feel a need for a little privacy or time to myself, I promise to be just as honest with you. I think this is going to be a great new chapter in our relationship."

5. *If there is a specific area of a parent's intrusion into your emotional life, be prepared to confront it firmly yet graciously.* Stay focused on the present-day situation. Avoid cluttering your communication with a lot of side issues and past grievances. Keep your communication brief and to the point. Be constructive rather than critical, and be as positive as possible.

For example: "Mom, I know you love me and you are concerned for my well-being, but I would appreciate it if you would not ask me any more questions about the people I'm dating." This statement affirms the parent's loving intention and is focused in the present and on the specific issue at hand. Bringing up side issues or past events only generates defensiveness, hurt, and conflict: "Why do you always ask me that? Everytime I go out with someone, you pump me for information! And while we're at it, it's none of your business where I go to church or what movies I go to either!" If you want to address other areas where you feel your parent violates your boundaries, wait until they arise, then deal with them singly and specifically. If you patiently make these little adjustments, one by one, it won't be long before you find that you have significantly "regrooved" your relationship with your parents into more healthy and productive patterns.

6. *Whenever you talk to your parents about redefining the boundaries of your relationship, reassure them that you still want them to be a part of your life.* "Dad," you might say, "I enjoy having you in my life as a friend and a father but not as a critic. If you're going to criticize the choices I make, I'm going to have to ask you to leave. If you're going to be positive and affirming, then you're welcome to stay."

Todd's mother had a habit of calling at about 10:30 or 11:00 at night, often interrupting Todd's sexual relationship with his wife, Sandi. At first, he tried ignoring the phone, but his mother was very persistent, and there's nothing that kills a romantic mood like twenty or thirty jingles from the bedside phone. Sandi suggested unplugging the phone at bedtime, but that didn't seem like a much better solution. After all, what if they forgot to plug it in again later?

Finally, Todd decided to face the problem directly and have a talk with his mother. "Mom, I love talking to you on the phone," he said, making sure he affirmed his mother up front, "but I'd appreciate it if you wouldn't call after 10:00 o'clock at night. Sandi and I like to keep those late-night hours special just for ourselves, okay?" Todd never had another problem with late-night phone calls, and his mother didn't feel that she was being cut off from him.

7. *Be aware that as you make these changes, you are going to lose some of the comfort and familiarity as well as the pain of enmeshment.* Be prepared to grieve that loss. Grieve for the sense of security and protection you once knew as an emotionally dependent child. Recognize that the feelings of sadness and depression you feel are a normal and temporary part of the changes you have made in your life. Those emotions will fade. And as they fade, you will feel a growing sense of confidence and security in your newfound status as a mature and independent adult.

CONTROL BOUNDARIES

Giselle's parents didn't like it when she chose to move from her hometown on the East Coast all the way out to California to attend a Christian college. Despite their pleading and tugging and all the brochures for East Coast colleges they shoved at her, Giselle persevered and made the move. For the next four years, her parents spent a fortune on long-distance calls and could have nearly bought their own airline for what they spent in coast-to-coast visits.

Just before graduation, Giselle phoned her parents with the news that she had met the man she was going to marry. Her parents first panic-stricken question was "Where will you live?" When she told them that her beau had a good job offer in southern California, her parents had a conniption! Giselle's mother broke into piercing, wailing sobs. Her father turned accusatory: "You see what you're doing to your mother? We've waited four long years for you to come home where you belong, and now you betray us like this! You remember this, young lady: there are a lot of eligible young men out there for you to marry, but you only have two parents— and you only have them for so long. If you really loved us, you would come right home after graduation. If you marry this man, then you might as well take a knife and cut our hearts out!"

Giselle's parents were controllers. They used guilt and manipulation in an attempt to control where their daughter lived and whom she married. Giselle worked hard to put healthy boundaries between herself and her parents' controlling grasp. In fact, that was specifically why she put an entire continent between herself and her parents throughout her college years. Giselle wanted to chart her own course in life, but it was not easy or painless.

Perhaps you can identify with Giselle. You may know from firsthand experience how hard it can be to break free of your parents' loving, well-intentioned, but ultimately smothering control.

As an adult, you have a duty and a right to make your own decisions regarding your career choices, your finances, your friends, your dating choices, your marital choice, your leisure time, where you choose to live, and how you choose to live. If you like, you can ask for the opinions and counsel of other people, including your parents, regarding these and other choices in your life. But no one, not even a parent, has the right to manipulate, coax, coerce, or otherwise try to control you and your choices. When your parents try to have a controlling role in these areas of your life, it's time to lay down some boundaries.

As you examine the need for control boundaries in your life, ask yourself the following questions:

1. *Do my parents control me—or do I allow my parents to control me?* We contribute to our own lack of boundaries in many ways. People often come to me saying, "I feel so helpless. My mother (or my father) controls me." But they have left an important factor out of the equation: their own responsibility. I try to get people to move from the statement "My parents control me" to "*I let* my parents control me." Once they are aware of their own participation in the problem, people begin to feel empowered and capable of solving the problem.

Charlie was in that position. "My parents have a big conflict going on," he told me, "and I'm caught in the middle. Both of them are tugging at me, trying to swing my allegiance to one side or the other. I'm stuck. There's just no way out." It's easy to see why Charlie felt trapped in this situation. His dad would take him aside and say, "Look, don't tell your mother I told you this, but . . ." And his mom would say, "Your father would be furious if he knew I was telling you this, but . . ." Poor Charlie thought he was responsible for resolving his parents' conflict. Why did he feel that way? Because both parents took him into their confidence and tried to make him their ally. So I asked Charlie, "Don't you see any options in this situation?"

"None," he said. "Solomon himself couldn't solve this one."

"Well," I said, "I agree that your parents have a pretty tough conflict to resolve. But your problem is really very simple, as I see it."

Charlie looked at me in astonishment. "How's that?"

"You have a problem only because you let your parents make it your problem. Charlie, it's not your problem. It's their problem. Let them solve it."

Charlie had to think about that for a couple weeks. But the next time I saw him, he told me he had solved his problem. "Mom and Dad each came to me again this past week," he said, "and both were still trying to get me to choose up sides. I told each of them, 'Look, I shouldn't be in the middle of this conflict between you two. This is something you have to solve for yourselves, so just leave me out.' They were both stunned that I would say such a thing. But they accepted it. I hope they find a way to work out their problem, but at least it's their problem now, not mine."

2. *What is the truly loving thing to do?* Is it truly loving toward your parent to allow him to continue acting like a dictator or a puppeteer? Is it truly loving to allow your parent to act in an infantile way, depending on you to meet his wants and needs? Or is it more loving to draw healthy boundaries, to create healthy understandings, to have healthy communication, and to build a healthy relationship? You don't have to think too hard about this one. You already know the answer.

3. *Am I a reactor—or an initiator?* In order to have healthy boundaries between yourself and an overprotective, controlling parent, you cannot be content to react. You must act. You must initiate. You must be proactive.

Maggie was a single woman in her late twenties. Maggie's mother called every Thursday night at 7:00. "How are you doing, Maggie?" she'd ask. "Are you eating right? Getting plenty of vegetables? Remember what too many Dove bars can do to your figure. Who are you dating these days? Is he a nice boy? Has he tried to get fresh with you? Do I know his parents? Are you going to church every Sunday? I hope you are keeping up with your feminine hygiene. Do you still get those bad cramps every month? Do you need any Midol? I have some extra. What kind of deodorant are you using, dear? I hope you're staying away from the ones with that aluminum whatchamacallit." And on and on and on.

Maggie was desperate for some way to escape this weekly cross-examination. So I offered a suggestion. I told her, "You say she calls every Thursday night at 7:00? Why don't you take the initiative and call her every Thursday night at 6:45. Ask your mother about her day. Show some interest in her

activities. I suspect she's just a little lonely, and the only reason she cross-examines you about your personal life is that
she doesn't know any other way to keep a conversation going.
If you ask her questions, I bet she'll feel comfortable talking
about her own day—and you'll be off the hot seat."

Maggie took my suggestions and took the initiative. And
since that day, there have been no more intrusive questions
from Maggie's mom.

Sometimes there is only one way to deal with a control-
prone parent: you have to confront her behavior. Confronting
doesn't mean picking a fight or letting your parents have it
right between the eyes. All you need to do is turn off the controlling behavior. This change can often be accomplished
without hurting your parents. The keys to effective confrontation are:

Be firm. Don't show hesitation or indecision. Decide ahead
of time where you want to draw your boundaries, and then
stick to them. Don't apologize for those boundaries. Just state
them clearly and firmly.

Be focused. Don't feel you have to supply reasons, ration-
ales, or arguments to bolster your position. Don't bring in ex-
traneous issues. Don't bring up the past. Confront one
behavioral issue at a time.

Be brief. Plan what you want to say, put it in as few sentences as possible, and stick to that plan. If your parents try to
engage you in an argument or raise side issues or past events,
don't get distracted. Just come right back to your planned
message, and restate it firmly and briefly.

Be calm. Don't get rattled. Don't let your parents control
your emotions. You be in control.

These are the principles Giselle practiced to deal with her
parents when they wanted to control her choice of whom to
marry and where to live. Even before she made the call, she
had an idea how her parents would respond, so she had her
countermoves planned in advance. When her mother broke

into wailing sobs and her father accused her of betraying them and "cutting their hearts out," Giselle paused to regain her composure. She didn't exactly feel calm, but she prayed for God's peace and focused on her planned statement.

"Mom, Dad," she said, "I love you, and I want to have a relationship with you. But I am an adult, and I will marry whom I choose to marry and live where I choose to live. I'll come home to visit, I'll write, I talk to you on the phone, I'll still be your daughter, but I will make my own decisions and live my own life."

Firm. Focused. Brief. Calm. She simply stated her *right* and her *intention* to make her own decisions. In that short speech, Giselle gave her parents nothing they could use as leverage to control her will. If she had offered excuses or arguments, they would have parried with counterarguments. If she had apologized for her decisions, they would have twisted her apologies into guilt. By staying firm, focused, brief, and calm, she retained control.

The boundary line had been indelibly, clearly drawn. Giselle's mother might wail. Her father might fume and smolder. But they would get over it. If they wanted to have a relationship with their adult daughter, they would have to get over it. That was not the last time Giselle had to confront her parents, but as they gradually learned that their relationship with Giselle would continue, their controlling behavior subsided.

TIME BOUNDARIES

Phil's dad is blind and in his seventies. He has lived with Phil's family ever since his wife died two years ago. He loves to regale Phil and his two teenage sons with stories of the old days. The problem is that Phil and his boys have lives of their own, and they don't always have time to be regaled. If they tell the old man they don't have time for his stories, he gets sullen and depressed and talks as if his life is over. So Phil wants to know, "How can I set time boundaries with my dad without making him feeling ignored and unwanted?"

Jill's mother phones most mornings at around 9 A.M., and wants to talk most of the morning away. Jill has a husband, three kids, and a ton of work to do. "Mom won't take a hint," says Jill. "I say, 'Oh, there goes the teakettle, gotta go!' Mom says, 'I'll wait.' I say, 'Oh, there's the doorbell, gotta go!' Mom says, 'I'll call you back in fifteen minutes.' Once, I tried something totally outrageous. I said, 'Oops, Mom, gotta go! My appendix just burst!' She just said, 'Don't be silly, dear, you had your appendix out when you were twelve.' I mean, nothing gets through to that woman! How can I set time boundaries with my mother without making her feel she's getting the brush-off?"

Here are some ways to have more clearly defined time boundaries in your relationship with your parents:

Look for the root cause of your parent's intrusiveness. In the case of Phil's father, the root cause was a sense that he was no longer needed or wanted or useful. He couldn't work, he couldn't help with the chores, he couldn't "earn his keep" around the house. All he had to offer anyone were his memories and his stories. Those stories were taking up Phil's time and his sons' time.

So Phil devised an ingenious and practical solution. He bought his father a tape recorder and encouraged him to put his stories on tape—to create an oral history for the family archives. Phil also knew that his younger son was taking typing in junior high and was also looking for ways to earn money, so Phil killed three birds with one stone: he had his son practice his typing skills and paid him a quarter a page to transcribe Grandpa's tapes. Before his father died, Phil had the stories printed up and bound in a book, which he distributed at the family reunion. Phil's dad was not only honored and praised for having produced a treasured oral history, but he felt useful and valued during what turned out to be the last few years of his life.

Set ground rules with parents who overstay (or over-phone) their welcome—and stick to those ground rules. Tell your parents at the beginning of the call whether it's a good time to talk and how long you can talk.

Jill learned that the key to limiting the intrusions of her mother's phone calls was to state at the outset, "I have fifteen minutes to talk, and then I have to go." When fifteen minutes was up, Jill firmly but cheerfully said good-bye. Sure, she felt guilty at first, but those misplaced guilt feelings were soon offset by her feelings of accomplishment as, for the first time in months, her house was spotless, her laundry was done, and her dishes were clean.

Be honest and unapologetic. Jill used to make excuses for trying to get off the phone: a whistling teapot, a ringing doorbell, even a burst appendix. Now she simply tells the truth: "Time's up, Mom. I've got to get back to work. Call me tomorrow morning and you can finish telling me about Aunt Elsie's funeral."

If you plan to impose a time boundary, give your parents a little advance warning, so they can get used to the idea. Examples: "I won't be able to stay as long at Christmas this year, Dad—just Christmas Day." Or, "Starting next month, I won't be able to take you grocery shopping each week—just once a month. I wanted to tell you now, so you can make other arrangements for the days I can't take you." Or "Mom, I can't go with you to the Crafts Festival this year. Why don't you see if Bonnie wants to go with you?"

Expect the worst. If you've just started setting time boundaries with your parents, don't expect your parents to rejoice. Don't let their crying or accusations or anger divert you from your course. Persevere. Eventually, they will accommodate themselves to the new, healthy, well-bounded relationship you are structuring.

If your parent generates conflict during visits or phone calls, set clear boundaries around issues and topics which lead to arguments. Tell your parents clearly, "If you come over, we will not discuss that issue." If the "forbidden topic" happens to come up anyway, just say, "We already agreed not to discuss that." Let that be your last word on the subject. Don't get drawn back into old, unproductive conflicts. Don't take the bait.

Determine your verbal countermoves in advance. Be prepared for manipulation and unwelcome intrusions. The intrusive parent should be dealt with in the same way as the controlling parent:

- *Be firm.*
- *Be focused.*
- *Be brief.*
- *Be calm.*

Find ways to spend positive, enjoyable time with your parents. Plan special family times with your parents for building relationships and making memories, such as a backyard barbecue, a birthday celebration, a home movie night. Show your parents they do not need to feel threatened by the new and healthy time boundaries you have laid down. When your parents see that you still love them and want to be with them, they will learn to accept the boundaries that you establish.

FINANCIAL BOUNDARIES

Randy's parents recently suffered a major financial reversal. Randy is not rich, but he is financially comfortable, so he told his dad he wanted to help them out with their living expenses. "How much will it take to get you by, Dad?" he asked. His dad named a figure that nearly stopped Randy's heart. "I-I guess I can do that, Dad," Randy stammeringly replied.

Since then, Randy has been steadily draining his own bank account to help his folks "get by." Yet his parents have continued to live in an $800,000 house, to take expensive Caribbean vacations, to buy lavish Christmas gifts—all with money Randy gave them. When Randy worked up the courage to ask his dad when they planned to scale back their life-style, his dad said, "Oh, I couldn't do that! Your mother would be so hurt!" Randy wants to set financial boundaries with his parents, but he doesn't know how to do so without hurting them.

Janine has the opposite problem: ever since she got her own job and her own apartment, she has remained dependent on money from home. She started working as a secretary in the San Francisco Bay area, making only $12,000 a year. The rent on her modest one-bedroom apartment consumed almost her entire take-home pay. So every month, her dad sent her an allowance. And that's exactly what he called it: an "allowance." Perhaps this had something to do with the fact that he still seemed to view and treat Janine as an adolescent—prying into her social life, her love life, and other private matters.

Janine felt trapped by a low-paying job and a high cost of living. She wanted to set boundaries with her dad, but she couldn't afford to cut the umbilical cord which tied her to Daddy's checkbook. As long as Daddy was paying the bills, Janine didn't feel she had the right to limit her father's intrusions into her life.

Money makes the world go 'round. When it comes from the hand of a controlling or enmeshed parent, money can be a powerful tool for keeping us from making changes in an unhealthy relationship. When it drains like water out of our bank account in order to keep needy, dependent parents afloat, money can become a major source of family tension and conflict.

One of the signs that we have achieved full and healthy adulthood is that our financial life is completely separate from that of our parents. This doesn't mean that parents can't help their children (or children help their parents) with an occasional gift or loan. Nor does it mean there is anything unhealthy about helping or caring for aging parents in one's home or through institutional care. But the normal situation in a healthy parent/adult-child relationship is for finances to be completely separate. To be a healthy, functional adult means:

- To take personal responsibility. You don't expect other people, including parents, to provide for you.
- To prefer to be uncomfortable, vulnerable, and even a little anxious about the future rather than to be dependent and enmeshed.
- To take risks and accept sacrifices in order to maintain your independence. If it means incurring a modest amount of debt or putting off that new stereo or bigger house for a year or two, then you do so.
- To strike a careful balance between independence and loving involvement with your parents. You don't disengage. You don't enmesh. You *balance*.
- To take more pride in your accomplishments than in your possessions and status symbols. You would rather earn a Ford Escort with your own efforts than have your parents hand you a Jaguar for free.
- To refuse to let the expectations and pressures of your parents, your spouse, your kids, or your friends push you into making dependent, imprudent decisions (such as overspending or accepting handouts). You stand up to pressure and make wise, mature, courageous decisions.
- To take the necessary steps to cure financial problems yourself. Find a new or extra job, cut back spending, put away credit cards, get credit counseling or psychological counseling to cure overspending habits, and so forth. You don't expect others to make up your shortfalls. You don't feel

entitled to other people's money. You want to make your own way.

If you wish to have a healthy, adult relationship with your parents, here are some important principles to keep in mind regarding financial boundaries:

1. *Whenever you accept money from your parents, you incur a debt.* Even if your parents did not have the slightest intention of using money as a means of controlling you, being indebted to your parents makes it harder for you to be honest with them, to confront them when necessary, to make decisions that conflict with their wishes, to define boundaries in other areas of your life, and to resist their intrusions and control. The debt may never be mentioned in so many words, but you will know, they will know you know, and you will know they know you know. Whenever you wish to negotiate as an adult, you will be at a disadvantage because you will feel like, and be perceived as, a dependent child who owes a debt to Mom and Dad.

2. *Whenever you accept money from your parents, you diminish your own self-esteem.* It is frustrating and self-defeating to keep going back to your parents for help. Most people who accept money from their parents, either in the form of emergency loans or in the form of regular allowance, tend to feel guilty and embarrassed. It is not something they talk about to their friends. They may even hide it from their own spouses. Adults who take money from parents often feel ashamed and inadequate.

3. *Loans from parents to adult children are frequently never repaid, and the debt goes on and on.* The bank can repossess your car or foreclose on your house if you don't make the payments. Sears and Exxon and MasterCard can fill your credit report with a lot of nasty black marks if you are late on your credit card payments. But Mom and Dad will keep on loving you no matter what, right? So who is always last in

line to get paid? You may have other creditors breathing down your neck right now, but if you owe a debt to your parents, you have a moral and ethical obligation to move them to the head of the line when you write your monthly checks.

4. *Your parents have no obligation to impoverish themselves on your behalf.* If you are in serious financial difficulty, facing a foreclosure or bankruptcy, think very carefully before asking your parents to bail you out. Can they afford it? Will you be dragging them down with you? Will you imperil their financial security in their retirement years by accepting money from them? Consider the possibility that it may be more responsible, ethical, and moral to take your medicine, whether it be an extra job, credit counseling, even bankruptcy, rather than endanger your parents' future.

5. *You have no obligation to impoverish yourself on your parents' behalf.* If your parents are in financial difficulty, you naturally want to help them any way you can. If you are in a position to help them, then perhaps you should. But before risking your own financial health to rescue your parents, take time to go over all the options with them. Sit down with them and ask them if the problem is that there is not enough income or that there are leaks in their bank account that could be plugged. Is their spending out of control? Are they "easy pickings" for con men? Do your parents give too much money to charities, churches, televangelists, and so forth? Are your parents spendaholics? Are they being continually fleeced by one of your ne'er-do-well siblings or other relatives? Are they in a house that is larger than they need and too expensive to maintain? Are they overinsured? Are they prone to making bad investments? By talking with your parents about their finances (or possibly referring them to an expert who can help them), it may be possible to avert financial disaster for your parents without having to write them a check.

6. *If you or your parents have trouble with spending, saving, investing, and indebtedness, seek professional help and counseling.* Your pastor or counselor can usually provide

help or direct you to the resources you need. Two very helpful sources of insight for Christians are Christian Stewardship Ministries, which offers family money management seminars nationwide, and Crown Ministries, Inc., which has small group meetings on family money management principles in churches across the country. For more information, contact your local church or contact these organizations directly.

Write or call:

Mr. Ken Smith
Christian Stewardship Ministries
10523 Main Street
Fairfax, Virginia 22030
(703) 591-5000

Crown Ministries, Inc.
530 Crown Oak Centre Dr.
Longwood, FL 32750
(407) 331-6000

THE KEY TO HEALTHY RELATIONSHIPS

Randy learned that he had to move out of the "rescuer" role with his parents. After a long and emotional confrontation with his parents, his mother and father agreed that they didn't have the right to endanger Randy's financial health for the sake of their country club life-style. They trimmed expenses, sold the $800,000 house, and moved from the posh and pricey East Bay area of California to the much less expensive (but genteel and enjoyable) life-style of Orlando, Florida. Randy's kids always look forward to their semi-annual visit to Grandma and Grandpa—and, of course, a few days at Disney World.

Janine, too, was able to define clear financial boundaries. She started with an aggressive job search, eventually landing an executive assistant position that raised her salary by 60 percent. Then she bought a secondhand computer and printer for $600, posted an ad on the student union bulletin board at the local university, and started typing term papers on the side. Then she told her dad to stop sending her an allowance. The checks kept coming for a couple months, but she scribbled, "VOID. THANKS BUT NO THANKS, DAD!" across the face of each check and sent it right back. Soon the checks stopped coming. And so did her father's intrusive questions into her private life. Janine was finally an adult. She was free.

And you can be too. You can change an unhealthy, entwined, enmeshed relationship into a mutually respectful friendship between equal adults. The key to healthy relationships is clear, well-defined boundaries. Face your issues courageously. Talk openly and honestly with your parents. Stake out your boundaries and guard them with your life.

Welcome to adulthood.

In the next chapter, we will look at practical ways to honor and love our parents, even when we don't feel like loving them.

8

How to *Really*
Love a Parent

"My father was an intimidating, domineering man," says Wendy, "and I disliked him intensely all my life. He never apologized for anything. He never admitted mistakes. He never told me he loved me or demonstrated affection for me. I spent my childhood and most of my adulthood either kowtowing to him or avoiding him.

"A couple of years ago, as I was approaching my mid-thirties, it occurred to me that it was time to change my attitude toward my father. I didn't want this kind of strained relationship to go on until he finally passed away, leaving me with a lot of unresolved feelings and regrets. One of us had to change, and it certainly wasn't going to be him, so it had to be me.

"My father was approaching the age of sixty, so for his birthday I decided to do something special for him. I sat down and forced myself to think of positive memories and character traits of my father that I could honestly affirm. I think that's the hardest thing I've ever done. It took a long time to think of sixty positive things to say about my dad. I mean, it's hard to think of sixty positive things to say about people you like!

"One of my hobbies is calligraphy, so the next thing I did was take two large sheets of parchment and list sixty of those memories and traits in flowing script, thirty on each sheet. I wrote a title over the top in blue ink with gold foil accents. On top of one sheet it says, 'For Your Sixtieth Birthday,' and on the other, 'Sixty Things I Love About You.' It starts out, 'Dear Daddy, here are sixty things I love about you, one for every year of your life.' And at the bottom of the second page, I signed my name, 'Your adoring daughter, Wendy.' I had the parchments matted and framed and gift-wrapped, and I gave them to him at his birthday party.

"Now, I didn't feel like an 'adoring daughter' while I did this. In fact, there were times when I thought, 'Why am I doing this? I don't even like this man!' But two things happened as a result of this gift I made for my dad. First, my attitude changed almost immediately. I began to see that my dad was a man with a lot of pain in his past. Underneath all that sarcasm and egotism and inflexibility was a scared, hurt little boy. I wondered what must have happened in his childhood that turned him into the kind of man he was. As I started to view him in this new way, I found that I was no longer able to dislike him anymore.

"The second amazing thing that happened was that my father actually changed! The old hardness and harshness seemed to soften. He became physically more affectionate, and he would actually say, 'I love you' right out of the blue. He never did that before!"

Wendy is living proof of the healing power of *love*. Unconditional love can redefine and restore a strained relationship. It can melt a hardened heart. It can radically change the lives of both the one who loves and the one who is loved. Wendy's experience demonstrates how important it is for us to find ways to really love our parents. We don't necessarily have to like them. We don't have to feel good about everything they have done to us. But regardless of the past, regardless even of problems and pain that continue in the present, we can make a choice to love our parents in realistic and practical ways.

We are not responsible for what our parents did to us, but we are responsible for our attitude and our behavior today. Once we understand what that means, as Wendy did, we become *empowered* and *impelled* to make positive changes in our relationship with our parents. This is an important and elevating principle!

People are continually amazed at the dramatic changes that can be brought about with a modest amount of effort and sacrifice. Frequently, all it takes to remake a relationship is a little creativity and caring. In the next few pages, we will explore some of the simple yet meaningful acts of caring that you can do to demonstrate unconditional, volitional love in these areas:

- **Service in the Small Things**
- **Service in Guarding Your Parents' Reputation**
- **Service in Allowing Your Parents to Serve You**
- **Service in Listening**

SERVICE IN THE SMALL THINGS

One of the most profound ways to love a parent is to always be ready to serve that parent; not in an enmeshed, guilt-ridden, obligated way, but through simple yet profound acts of love, freely and willingly offered.

Report to your parents your small and large daily successes and achievements. Most parents are interested and appreciate being involved in the joys of your life.

Express gratitude and appreciation for a gift or an experience they gave you long ago: "Remember that trip we took to the Grand Canyon? I still have great memories of that trip." Or "I'll never forget how you lent me your new car so I could take my date to the prom." Or "You know, I still wear that beautiful necklace you gave me for my college graduation. Thanks again."

Send your parents gifts for no particular reason, on no particular occasion. Try to be creative rather than lavish. A wallet-size picture in a frame that's also a refrigerator magnet. A special video of their grandkids, dubbed and edited together from the last five or ten years' worth of home videos. A handmade memento. A photo album filled with pictures and clippings or a matted 8x10 photo of your parents sharing a moment with their grandkids. Theater or symphony tickets. Let your imagination roam.

Show your parents you are thinking of them. Send them newspaper clippings, cartoons, and articles you know they would enjoy.

Pray for your parents. Thank God for them. Tell them you continually remember them in your prayers.

SERVICE IN GUARDING YOUR PARENTS' REPUTATION

One of the most common complaints I hear from my clients about their parents is, "My mom and dad are always criticizing me and bad-mouthing me!" The truth is that bad-mouthing often cuts both ways. People easily fall into bad habits when there is strain in a relationship: backbiting, complaining, griping, grumbling, accusing, blaming. And it's a lot easier to recognize bad-mouthing when others do it to you than when you do it to others. The best way to break this bad habit is to substitute a good habit. Call it "good-mouthing."

Whenever you talk about your parents with other people, even your spouse or other confidants, practice finding something good to say about them. Try focusing on the things they did right (however few and far between) rather than on the wrongs they did. Try to focus on their strengths rather than on their weaknesses. Try to focus on their virtues rather than on their sins. In time, you will repattern your communication habits and the way you think and feel about your parents.

Treat your parents' reputation as a precious asset to be protected and cherished. Avoid complaining about your parents' weaknesses or faults in the presence of friends and acquaintances.

Make a point of telling your friends and acquaintances about your parents' achievements and virtues, both past and present. Find reasons to be proud of your parents.

SERVICE IN ALLOWING YOUR PARENTS TO SERVE YOU

Again, the focus is on the small things. When you let your parents serve you in simple, practical ways, they feel needed, useful, and most of all, loved. Some examples:

- Ask your parents for advice, help with household projects, baby-sitting, and so forth.
- Seek out their memories and stories of "the old days."
- Seek their opinions on small matters: "What do you think of this color on me? Should I wear this to the party? Which item do you think would make a better wedding gift for cousin Alice? Do you think the picture looks better on this wall or that wall?" Let them know you care what they think.

SERVICE IN LISTENING

Another common complaint I hear from my clients about their parents is, "They never listen to me!" Sometimes my response to that complaint is, "Do you ever listen to them?" Often, the door of communication is shut and barred from *both* sides, not just the parents' side. If the adult child will take the initiative to be warm, receptive, and nonjudgmental, the parents will often take the cue and unbar the door from their side.

We often fail to realize how poor our own listening skills are. But it should come as no surprise. Since we learned our listening skills from our parents, it is only natural that if they are not good listeners, we might not be very good listeners ourselves.

Here are some practical tips on how to demonstrate your love through listening:

- As you listen to your parent, give her positive, encouraging feedback through steady eye contact, a warm smile, an occasional nod of enthusiasm, and open, welcoming body language and facial expressions.
- Listen for the *feelings* communicated beneath the words. The facts of your parent's message are not as important as his emotional response to those facts.
- In your own words, reflect back to your parent what you hear her saying. Nothing makes a person feel she has been heard like hearing her own thoughts and feelings accurately mirrored back to her.
- Ask questions which show you are engaged and interested in what your parent has to say.
- Avoid daydreaming or becoming distracted.
- Avoid responding with a message of your own. Particularly avoid "topping" your parent's story or taking over the conversation. Concentrate on being receptive rather than talkative. Avoid mentally rehearsing what you are going to say next.
- Avoid reading anything into what your parent says or projecting your own bias on his message. Try to listen to what he is *really* saying, not what you assume he is saying because of conflicts or circumstances of the past.

- Avoid interrupting or showing impatience with your parent. Let her finish her own sentences.
- Avoid making responses that could cause your parent to feel defensive or embarrassed.
- Avoid arguments over unimportant issues.

Focus on these skills, practice them, and turn them into habits. In most cases you will find that your efforts will pay dividends in a better relationship with your parents. There are few better ways to communicate love than by listening.

What if you don't *feel* like doing any of these things? What if you don't *feel* loving toward your folks? Don't let that stop you. There's an old saying: "You've got to fake it till you make it." Even if you don't feel like loving your parent, you can still *will* yourself to do loving acts of service and kindness. In time, especially if your parent responds favorably, the feelings may follow.

And wouldn't *that* be a surprise!

THE TWO HUNDREDTH HUG

In his book *Making Peace with Your Parents*, Dr. Harold H. Bloomfield relates the story of the last part of his father's life. Bloomfield was on a book promotion tour when word reached him that his father was in the hospital, diagnosed with a particularly malignant form of cancer. Bloomfield caught the next plane home. He was acutely aware of a great deal of unfinished business he had with his father. His father was a cold and distant man who never displayed emotion, who could never tell those close to him that he loved them. Bloomfield's relationship with his father had always been strained. "He had always been my father," Bloomfield recalls, "but I felt that I barely knew him as a person."

As he entered the hospital and made his way to his father's room, Bloomfield decided that it was time to change the disengaged relationship they had lived with for so many years. "I made up my mind," he relates, "that I was going to reestablish closeness with each of my parents. Keeping them at arm's length was no longer what I wanted."

He found his father in a hospital bed in intensive care, hooked up to tubes and monitors. He had lost considerable weight, and his skin was jaundiced. The doctors offered slim hope for recovery. Bloomfield approached him, and the first words from his mouth were words of honest feeling: "Dad," he said, "I really love you." And he leaned over, reached his arms around his father and gave him a hug. His father went stiff as a board. He looked shocked, even scared. Showing affection was just something he had never done before.

Bloomfield said, "C'mon, Dad, I really want to give you a hug." And he hugged his father again. This time, his father was even more stiff than before! Bloomfield could sense a cold resentment building inside him. His love was being rejected! He almost gave his father a chewing out on the spot for being a stiff, cold-hearted old man.

But then a change came over Bloomfield. He thought about his father's formal, Germanic upbringing. He remembered that his father was probably taught as a young boy to close off his feelings in order to be a man. A lifetime of habit and conditioning, Bloomfield realized, cannot be changed in a few moments on a deathbed. With that realization came a new determination. He had come here to demonstrate love for his father, and he was going to demonstrate love for his father!

"C'mon, Dad," he said, "put your arms around me. Now squeeze. That's it. Now again, squeeze. Very good!" And he proceeded to teach his father how to give a hug. And that was just the first of many hugging lessons. Day after day, Bloomfield returned to his father's bedside. Day after day, he leaned over and gave his father a hug. Day after day, his father was as stiff and awkward as a board.

"It took months," says Bloomfield, "before his rigidness gave way and he was able to let the emotions inside him pass through his arms to encircle me. I knew we were succeeding because more and more we were relating out of care and affection. Around the two hundredth hug, he spontaneously said out loud, for the first time I could ever recall, 'I love you.'"

For Harold Bloomfield, his father's cancer was both a *tragedy* and an *opportunity*; an opportunity for growth and change in his relationship with his father and indeed with both of his parents. Bloomfield was even able to use his skills as a psychotherapist to assist his parents in working out some of the long-buried issues and resentments that had festered inside each of them over the years. By the time his father died, Bloomfield recalls, "I felt that my father was my oldest and dearest friend."

Perhaps Harold Bloomfield's love was the key to an amazing gift his father received, the gift of *time*. For although the doctors had predicted he would only live another three to six months, Bloomfield's father survived his cancer for *over four years*—four beautiful, reconciled, joyous years.

"Those four years of peace with my parents made a tremendous difference in my life," Bloomfield concludes. "From healing my resentments and sharing more love with my parents, I also gained inner peace."[1]

Genuine love is not a feeling. It is an attitude choice. It is a behavioral choice. Loving your parents unconditionally doesn't mean excusing the past. But it does mean living in the present and working to build a better future.

Learning to love the people who raised you—and even the people who hurt you—in simple, practical ways is one of the most courageous, healthy, and *adult* things any human being can do. It is a gift you give your parents. But even more, it is a gift you give to God.

And to yourself.

In the next chapter we will examine the special problems and issues of relating to parents-in-law.

9

Do I Have to Love My In-Laws?

Lisa's mother-in-law, Victoria, always babied her son when he was a child. After her son was grown and married, she expected his wife to baby him too. "I hate to see my son working so hard," said Victoria during one unannounced visit. (Lisa thought of these surprise visits as "inspections.") "He works hard all week long, and then you make him scrub the toilet and the shower and do all the vacuuming."

"I don't *make* him do anything," Lisa replied, seething inside. "It was as much his decision as mine that we would share the housework. He just happens to be a very thoughtful husband."

"Yes, I raised him to be thoughtful," said Victoria, "although sometimes I wonder if Mark isn't too thoughtful for his own good. The poor dear works such long hours to provide a good living for you . . ."

"Mark doesn't 'provide' for me," Lisa replied, barely keeping the lid on her anger. "You forget that there are *two* breadwinners around here, and I work as hard and earn as much as he does."

"Well, dear," Victoria countered with a sly and patronizing smile, "perhaps you should spend less time winning the bread and more time baking it. As you pointed out, Mark is very thoughtful. Too thoughtful to come right out and tell you that he'd rather come home at night to a real wife, not an over-ambitious career woman in a silk suit and floppy tie. Don't you think it's time you decide to settle down and be a wife to my son and start bearing him some children? You know, someday that biological clock of yours—well, I've probably said too much already. But I only said it for your own good. Just think it over, dear. I'm sure you'll agree I'm right."

Of course, the only thing Lisa agreed with was that Victoria had indeed said too much. This harangue was only one among many intrusive, abrasive, absolutely infuriating encounters Lisa had with her mother-in-law. Lisa loved her husband and enjoyed the life they had made together, but Lisa didn't know how much longer she could withstand the barbed tongue of her husband's mother.

"I always believed I was supposed to honor Mark's parents just like I honor and love my own," Lisa told me. "But how can I honor this woman? I can barely keep from belting her! What am I supposed to do?"

UNPACKING THE "BAGGAGE"

In-laws are a case unto themselves.

In-laws (particularly mothers-in-law) have been grist for the comedy mill ever since time began, and it's not hard to see why. The most surefire jokes are the ones in which we recognize reality. And the reality that I often encounter in my counseling practice is that a lot of people have serious, agonizing problems with their in-laws. And despite the jokes that are told about in-laws, these problems are no laughing matter to those who struggle with the pain.

Greg and Dorie had been married over twenty-five years. In all that time, Greg had never gotten along with Dorie's parents. They continually criticized him, gave him unwanted advice, and, even after all those years, compared him with some of Dorie's old boyfriends. The only way Greg could cope with the situation was to withdraw. Whenever Dorie's folks came to visit, he found an excuse to be someplace else. Dorie kept trying to coax Greg into being more involved with her parents. "Can't you just ignore the things they say and try to be nice to them?" she pleaded. "After all, you're a Christian, and Christians are supposed to love people no matter what. And they're my parents. If you really love me, you should find some way to love my parents." So Greg came to me and asked, "What should I do? Do I have to maintain a relationship with people who continually put me down and make me uncomfortable?"

Trisha's mother-in-law, Grace, was a very needy, dependent woman in her late seventies. Grace was also rude, cantankerous, demanding, and utterly unpleasant to be around. Grace had a self-centered daughter who refused to lift a finger to help her. And Trisha's husband was working so many hours trying to get his new computer store off the ground that he was simply no help at all. So the entire load of caring for Grace fell on—who else?—Trisha.

Every week, Trisha drove Grace to various doctors, to the grocery store, and to church (Sunday morning and evening, plus Wednesday night prayer meeting). She also cleaned Grace's house and did her laundry. And through it all, she had to listen to the woman's continuous complaining, criticizing, and nagging. When Trisha came to my office, she immediately broke down in tears. "I can't take it anymore. I'm breaking under the strain. I wish that nasty old woman would up and die!"

Bernie had an unusual in-law problem. Whenever he visited his wife's parents for dinner, he was invariably seated next to his mother-in-law. Often as he was about to take his first bite of the dinner, she would reach out and grab his arm, stopping the fork from reaching his mouth. "Now, Bernard," clucked Mother Hen, "that bite is too hot! We mustn't eat our food until it has had time to cool!" Bernie found her behavior amusing but also a little embarrassing. "After all," he says, "I'm a forty-four-year-old man! Shouldn't I be the judge of what goes in my mouth and when?"

Even in the best of marriages, partners must adjust to in-laws. When you marry, you don't just marry your spouse, you marry an entire family. You are going to be spending a lot of time with these people. Holidays. Reunions. Vacations. Visits in your home and in theirs. You will be rubbing elbows with these people for the rest of your life, and sometime, sooner or later, you can expect one or more of those elbows to give you a jab in the ribs. You can expect one or more of these unpleas-antries:

- Petty annoyances
- Unwelcome intrusions
- Criticism
- Advice-giving
- Withdrawal, silence, and "freezing out"
- Barbed jokes and snide comments
- Emotional outbursts
- Conflict

In every marriage, two people come together, each with at least a couple of decades of allegiances built up toward his or her own family of origin. There is a built-in asymmetry to the relationship which often pits the parents and their adult child against the adult child's spouse. Clearly, this situation creates enormous pain for the spouse. But it also creates massive emotional pressures and conflicts in the adult child. He may want to be loyal to his spouse, but the parents have such a strong and intimidating grip on the adult child's loyalties that is very difficult for him to resist.

Added to this dynamic is the fact that the adult child often brings a lot of unexamined attitudes and assumptions into the marriage from the family of origin. Let's call these attitudes and assumptions *baggage*. This baggage contains expectations, traditions, values, beliefs, and habits. To have a healthy marriage relationship, baggage should be unpacked and sorted through. Some of the contents may be kept while some items should be discarded. The couple should agree on which items to keep and which to get rid of in order to create a workable, mutually agreeable synthesis of expectations, traditions, values, beliefs, and habits.

Unfortunately, many couples never consciously go through the baggage-sorting process. They never stop to objectively examine the attitudes they grew up with. They assume that the way they grew up is the "right" way and that their spouse's family had "funny" ideas and "weird" ways of doing things. It is easy to see how, when the adult child's baggage comes in conflict with that of her spouse, she can easily form an alliance with parents against the spouse: "This is the way we've always believed and done things. Obviously, the way you and your family believe and do things is wrong and ridiculous." This attitude is a prescription for marital disaster.

Rex's father is a male chauvinist. He's not a bad guy, really, but he loves to make remarks about "keeping women in their place." He loves to antagonize Rex's wife, Kelly, by saying to his son (loudly enough so that she can hear), "You ought to treat Kelly the same way I treated your mother: keep her barefoot and pregnant! They all gripe and groan and spout that Gloria Steinem bilge, but inside every woman there's a meek little wifey who wants to be kept and protected. Haw, haw, haw!"

Rex saw how much Kelly hated his father's talk. Even though she wasn't a radical feminist, she still felt insulted and put down by her father-in-law's Neanderthal attitudes. But instead of taking his dad aside and telling him to cool it, Rex *joined* his dad and chimed in with a few Archie Bunker style one-liners of his own. Rex had grown up all his life listening to his dad's chauvanistic remarks about women, and he had never bothered to unpack that baggage. So he aligned himself with his father, deeply offending his wife. That's a dangerous risk to take with a marriage.

Kevin and Lauren have been married just a little over a year. Lauren was raised in a very small town where everybody knew each other and where neighbors and church friends often walked into her parents' house without knocking. Kevin was raised in a big city where people kept their doors locked and their windows barred and where visitors had to identify themselves at the security gate before being allowed onto the premises. These differences between Kevin's baggage and Lauren's baggage created noticeable conflict in their marriage. Kevin was aggravated at Lauren's parents, whom he characterized as rude, boorish, and intrusive. "I never know when I step into the shower," he complained, "if I'm going to be greeted by your mother when I step out!" Lauren, meanwhile, was annoyed with Kevin's parents, whom she described as "a couple of cold, snobbish hermits who make us park our car outside the front gate and show three forms of I.D. before they'll let us say hello!" In order to resolve these differences, Kevin and Lauren needed to unpack their baggage and begin to understand the different geographies, traditions, and cultural assumptions that they each came from and were still operating with.

In many cases of in-law trouble, however, the problem of family-of-origin baggage is compounded by problems in the in-law's personality. A controlling parent, for example, is likely to turn out to be an equally controlling parent-in-law.

BREAKING THE GRIP OF A CONTROLLING IN-LAW

Let's take another look, for example, at the case of Lisa, who was tortured by the sharp-tongued criticism and advice-giving of her mother-in-law, Victoria. Not only did Victoria inflict her family's traditions and values on Lisa ("In our family, wives do not have careers. They scrub and bake and make babies"), but she also inflicted her controlling personality on

Lisa, using her barbed criticisms in an attempt to coerce Lisa into doing things her way. In order to resolve this problem with her Dictator-Parent-in-Law, I helped Lisa develop a three-pronged strategy. Here is what she did:

First, she recognized that since she was an adult equal with Victoria, she did not have to be intimidated or bullied by Victoria's criticism. She was free to simply ignore Victoria and her comments. This built her confidence and enabled her to let some of the less sharp comments bounce harmlessly off.

Second, she talked honestly with her husband Mark and asked him to align himself with her in trying to put an end to his mother's intrusive, controlling behavior. He agreed that his primary loyalty was to Lisa, and he agreed to tell Victoria that he and Lisa were making their own choices and that Victoria had no right to interfere with their decisions. As expected, this did not stop Victoria's intrusions. It only forced her to be more subtle in the way she tried to pressure Lisa to change.

Third, Lisa practiced asserting her independence firmly, confidently, and calmly. She needed to convey to Victoria that she and Mark were in control of their lives and would not yield that control to Victoria or anyone else. When Victoria brought up a subject such as their life-style and career choices, Lisa told her, "That is an area I choose not to discuss with you." She did not argue any particulars with Victoria, she simply closed the subject. If Victoria persisted, Lisa repeated her position: "As I said before, I choose not to discuss that with you." If Victoria persisted a third time, Lisa simply remained silent until Victoria became embarrassed by the silence and changed the subject.

Victoria's intrusions and barbed comments never entirely stopped, but they did subside to a level that Lisa felt comfortable dealing with. Today, Lisa feels empowered to deal with any future intrusions and considers her mother-in-law problems to be essentially resolved.

DO I HAVE TO SPEND TIME WITH MY IN-LAWS?

Greg's problem with Dorie's parents was similar in some ways to Lisa's problem. Dorie's parents continually barraged Greg with criticism, unwanted advice, and comparisons to Dorie's old boyfriends even though Greg and Dorie were in their forties and had been married over twenty-five years! Obviously, if Dorie's parents had not learned to accept Greg by this time, they never would. So Greg solved the problem by simply making himself scarce whenever his in-laws came to visit. He'd hole up in his woodshop or find some excuse to be out of the house.

Dorie and Greg came to me, wanting me to help them resolve this issue. Should Greg, as a Christian, try to be more involved with his in-laws and more tolerant of their verbal warfare against him, or should he simply go on avoiding them?

"Greg, let me ask you this," I said. "How do you feel about Dorie's parents? Are you bitter? Resentful?"

He thought about the question for a moment, then said, "No. I really don't think I am. They are just going to be the way they are, and I've pretty much accepted that. There was a time when I tried to argue with them or confront them or get them to accept me, but when it became clear they weren't going to change, I just thought it made more sense to steer clear. But I think I've forgiven them, and I don't feel I hold a grudge against them."

"Dorie," I said, "does Greg ever complain about your parents? Does he talk about them to other people and tear down their reputation? Do you think he holds any resentment against them?"

"No," she said. "He doesn't do any of that. If he ever talks about my parents, he always speaks favorably of them. I think he does that out of his love for me, and I really appreciate that. I just wish he could be more involved with my folks when they come over to visit."

"Because?"

"Well, because they're my family. I just like to have all my family together sometimes—my parents, my children, my husband, the people I care about."

"It seems to me," I observed, "that Greg has an obligation to honor your parents, to avoid sinning against them, to avoid slandering them, to avoid holding bitterness against them in his heart. And from what I'm hearing, it seems that Greg is doing all of that. But is Greg required to maintain an involved relationship with people who continually attack him and insult him? I don't think so. Dorie, I'd like you to consider the possibility that the best solution in this situation is the one Greg has chosen. He can continue to avoid a relationship with your parents—a relationship which would be damaging to him emotionally—and you are free to continue a relationship with your parents."

With the insight Dorie gained by talking through the dynamics of this relationship, she came to the conclusion that Greg had chosen the best possible compromise. The two of them agreed to continue this course.

CREATIVE SOLUTIONS

Trisha's in-law problem, you'll recall, involved a needy, dependent, utterly unpleasant mother-in-law named Grace. Trisha was required to provide taxi service and cleaning service for Grace because Grace's own children were either unable or unwilling to help out. Trisha was so burdened and exhausted from taking care of this woman that she actually wished her mother-in-law would die. And then, of course, she felt guilty for that! When she came to my office, Trisha had no hope that a solution could be found. As it turned out, however, we were able to work out some creative solutions to Trisha's problem in just a few counseling sessions.

One solution we tried involved confronting Grace's daughter (Trisha's husband's sister) and attempting to convince her to shoulder some of the workload. The daughter, however, was determinedly self-centered and irresponsible. She had plenty of spare time and a car to help transport her mother around town, but as long as Trisha was doing it all, why should she bother? Trisha and her husband did convince her, however, to chip in some money to hire a maid to do Grace's cleaning and laundry.

The next solution we tried was even more productive. A little research turned up some community services that Trisha's mother-in-law could access so that she could get around without Trisha's help. The local HandiRide transportation service whould take her to her doctor appointments for a very modest fare, and a shop-and-delivery service would do Grace's shopping for her and deliver the groceries to her door. Grace's church provided free transportation to Sunday and Wednesday services for the elderly and handicapped; all it took was a phone call.

Trisha's mother-in-law was resistant to these changes, and she had plenty of excuses and accusations ready to keep from having to make the adjustment: "I don't want to ride with a bunch of strangers! It'll be inconvenient! It'll be too expensive! You just don't love me anymore!" But Trisha and her husband remained firm: "We love you, Mom, but Trisha can't continue doing everything for you. She's exhausted, and she can't get her own work done. If you love us, then you'll be willing to use these services to make life easier for Trisha." Grace moped and grumped and griped, but eventually, grudgingly, she came around.

Bernie, the forty-four-year-old man whose mother-in-law grabbed his arm because his food was too hot, came up with an equally creative solution to his in-law problem. One time when Bernie and his wife were invited to his in-laws' home for dinner, he was again seated next to his wife's mother. After the food was blessed, Bernie took his soup spoon and dipped it into the steaming bowl of lobster bisque in front of him. Right on cue, he felt his mother-in-law's touch at his arm. "That's very hot, Bernard!"

"No problem," said Bernie. He reached into his coat pocket and pulled out a small battery-operated "personal cooling fan" he had purchased at Radio Shack. With a flourish, he turned the fan on and held it over his spoonful of soup, then put the soup in his mouth and made an elaborate show of savoring it.

Everyone at the table burst into laughter. Bernie's mother-in-law reddened slightly, but then she joined in the laughter. And she never grabbed his arm again.

Sometimes it takes tough talk and tough love to deal with in-laws. Other times it just takes a little creativity.

NO DEFENDER

Hannah, a woman in her thirties, came into my office feeling visibly frustrated and depressed. "I don't know what to do about my husband Dave and his parents," she said. "Dave and I have been married ten years. I have tried to be friendly and outgoing to his parents, I've given them three beautiful grandchildren, I've been a good wife to their son, and still they refuse to accept me. At family gatherings, they refuse to speak to me. When I initiate a conversation with them, they respond in monosyllables and turn away."

Hannah related to me the history of her relationship with Dave's parents. She had become a Christian a couple of years after they were married, and a few months later she led Dave to Christ. Dave's parents, who came from an unchurched background, seemed to feel threatened by the change in Dave and Hannah. They nicknamed their daughter-in-law "Holy Hannah" and ridiculed her for turning their son into a "Jesus freak."

One night, Hannah went into her children's bedroom to

read them a Bible story and pray with them before bedtime, but she couldn't find the children's Bible storybook. When she asked her kids where the book was, they said, "Grandpa took it when he was here today. He said, 'Your momma is always reading you that Bible junk. She wants to turn you all into a bunch of sissy preachers.' Then he gave us *this* to read." It was a comic book called *The Punisher*.

When Hannah phoned Dave's father and asked about the Bible storybook, he denied even touching it. "Sure, I gave them the comic book, but I don't know what they did with the Bible storybook," he said. Hannah could hear the chuckle in his voice. "Looks like all that religious propaganda isn't doing those kids any good anyway. They lie just like little heathen kids." The Bible storybook never turned up.

"You want to know how ridiculous those people are?" Hannah asked me. "They blame me for every little thing that goes wrong in Dave's life. Last week, Dave's company car blew an engine while he was on a sales trip, about a hundred miles from home. The oil pressure light came on, and he drove it another two miles down the freeway, looking for a service station. Of course, there's no better way to blow an engine than to drive it without oil, and that's exactly what my husband did. His parents and his brother and sister-in-law were at our house that night and Dave was telling them about it. Dave's dad pointed right at me and said, 'Well, there's your problem, son. You shouldn't let that woman drive your car!'

"I was furious! I said, 'I'll have you know that I have never even ridden in Dave's company car, much less driven it!' Well, that made his day, seeing me so angry. He grinned and chuckled, and he said, 'Well now, honey, seems to me you *must* have driven it! 'Cause I taught my son how to take proper care of a car, and a three-year-old car doesn't just blow an engine for no reason at all. For that to happen, a car has to be abused.'

"I said, 'Dave abused that car by driving it two miles down the freeway without any oil in it! He told me so himself!'

Dave's dad just chuckled again and said, 'Simmer down there, girl! Why don't you just admit that you borrow the keys sometimes when Dave doesn't know it?'

"By then, I realized he didn't believe a word he was saying. He was just needling me like he always does, but the more he laughed at me, the more I sputtered and fumed and the more foolish I looked. He was in complete control of the situation. I looked around the room at Dave's mom and his brother and sister-in-law, and they were all grinning at me, just like his Dad. And Dave didn't say one word to defend me. It's always like that. And I just can't take it anymore."

Clearly, Hannah had a major problem with her in-laws. But there was an even more basic problem at the core of her pain: her husband Dave let her take all this abuse alone. He would not defend his wife against his parent's attacks.

DEFENDING THE SAFETY ZONE

Remember the "hierarchy of priorities" graph from chapter 7? It shows how our loyalties and priorities are to be ordered:

God	**Highest priorities**
Spouse	
Children	
Family of Origin (Parents)	↑
Fellow Christians	
Neighbors	**Lowest priorities**

Hannah's husband Dave had fractured that hierarchy of priorities. He had placed loyalty to his family of origin over loyalty to his own spouse. This is a common problem that many couples have. From both a biblical and psychological point of view, however, it is absolutely necessary for the adult child to invest his loyalties in his spouse, not his parents. A boundary—let's call it a *safety zone*—must surround the marriage relationship. All intrusions into that safety zone, including *parental* intrusions, must be fended off for the good of the marriage. Dave and Hannah needed to agree that their marriage relationship was primary. In the traditional words of the marriage ceremony, they needed to leave father and mother and, forsaking all others, cleave only to each other.

Over the next few weeks I met with both Hannah and Dave. From his first session in counseling, Dave readily admitted that he had been wrong in failing to defend Hannah against his parents' attacks, but he didn't know how he should respond. I asked him, "Why do you suppose your parents keep attacking her so relentlessly?"

"That's easy," said Dave. "They want to split us up. They won't be happy until Hannah and I are divorced. I think Mom and Dad want me to get rid of Hannah and be their little boy again."

"How do you feel about that?"

"It makes me mad. I hate those mind games my dad plays with Hannah. He can be pretty cruel. He used to pull that stuff on me when I was growing up. The thing is, I don't know how to fight him. I don't know what to say."

"You've made a good start by recognizing the problem," I said. "It sounds like you know what you *should* do and what you *want* to do. Now you just need to know *how* to do it. You need some workable strategies."

His face brightened. "Exactly! I need a strategy! What should I do?"

We got to work and hammered out a strategy together. The three of us agreed that Dave needed to be the spokesman. They were his parents, and he had to confront their behavior. We did some role-playing, and we rehearsed some verbal moves and countermoves. I wanted Dave to be fully prepared for the onslaught of anger, accusation, and scathing remarks he was sure to get from his parents, particularly from his dad.

The next night, Dave called his parents and invited them

over. "We've got to talk about something," he told them. "I'll tell you what it's all about when you get here."

His parents arrived about twenty minutes later. When Dave's dad walked in the door, there was a sour look of annoyance on his face. He said, "All right, son, what's this all about?"

Dave indicated a couple chairs for his mother and father, then he sat down on the sofa next to Hannah and put his arm around her. She was trembling. "It's about the way you treat my wife, Dad. You and everyone in the family. I asked you over to tell you that it is going to stop right now."

Dave's father went into his amused good ol' boy routine. "Why, son," he chuckled, "I haven't got the foggiest idea what you are talking about!"

"Yes, you do," said Dave. And he proceeded to recount several recent episodes as his father's smile faded and his face darkened. His mother's face, by contrast, seem to grow pale.

"*You* put him up to this," the older man grumbled threateningly, pointing an accusing finger at Hannah.

"Look, Dad," Dave responded forcefully, "I've hated the way you and the family have treated Hannah for years. But until tonight, I haven't been man enough to do anything about it. But that's all changed. Dad, when you said that Hannah 'put me up to this,' that was an insult to me. No one controls me. Hannah has never controlled me, and you won't control me anymore. What I'm telling you tonight is only what I should have told you years ago. I'm not letting you and the family mistreat my wife anymore. I don't want to ever hear you say another word against her. You either take both of us, or you get neither. Those are the rules."

Dave's mother said nothing. She just sat with a stricken look on her face. Dave's father was silent for several long seconds, his jaw clenching and unclenching, while a big vein pulsed at his temple. Finally, he turned to Hannah and sneered, "Well, missy, I hope you're proud of yourself. Turning a man's son against him this way. You sneaking little . . ."

Dave interrupted him in mid-obscenity. "That's it, Dad," he said firmly yet calmly. "Get out of that chair and get out of my house."

"*What?!*" Dave's father's jaw dropped open. So did his mother's.

"You just broke the rules, Dad," Dave explained, sounding much more strong and resolute than he felt inside. "So I want you to leave my house. But before you go, understand this: Hannah's never turned me against you. She's always tried to reach out to you and make peace with you. The only one who can turn me against you is *you*. You're welcome in my house whenever you learn to treat my wife with respect. Until you do, well, there's the door."

Stunned, speechless, and scarcely believing what they were hearing, Dave's parents left the house. There were other confrontations in the years that followed, but eventually Dave's parents, as well as the rest of his family, got the message. There were new rules, and those rules were enforced.

Dave's family never became warmly affectionate toward Hannah but they did learn to respect the clear boundary line that Dave had drawn around his marriage relationship. Hannah's in-law problems were, for the most part, resolved. But she couldn't have resolved them by herself. Her husband was the key to the solution.

Sometimes, troublesome in-laws can be converted into treasured members of the family. But even when they can't be changed into loving and lovable people, they can still be taught to recognize and respect your boundaries.

In the next chapter, we will look at the "gray" areas of our parents' lives—the special challenges we face as our parents grow older.

10

"Gray" Areas—The Special Problems of Aging Parents

"**M**y mother always talked about what a wonderful life she had," recalls Judy. "She was a bubbly, joyful Christian who made other people feel happy just being around her. She had what she called a 'storybook childhood, a storybook romance, and a storybook life.' She was seventeen when she married my father, the first man she ever loved, and for sixty years they were very happily married.

"After Father died, Mother's health began to decline. She seemed to lose interest in life. She pulled out of her clubs and church activities. Before, she had always seemed so youthful and energetic—people usually guessed her to be ten or fifteen years younger than she really was. But as she grieved Father's death, she seemed to age almost overnight.

"She was having a lot of trouble sleeping, so the doctor prescribed some pills to help her sleep. One night she took too many, and she never woke up. The coroner called it an 'accidental overdose,' but I just don't know. The question of why my mother died still haunts me, and so does another question: Why, after seventy-seven years of a 'storybook life' did she have to end her days in such misery and depression?"

There's no satisfactory answer to Judy's question. But we do know that old age can be "the golden years" for many people and a time of sorrow and pain for others. It is a golden time for those who have acquired the wisdom and perspective that can come from spending sixty, seventy, or even more years of fruitful living. I've known many senior adults who were able to say, "These are the best years of my life!" They are people who, having already lived a long and rewarding life, still have a lot of living to do and much to look forward to.

Yet it is inevitable that a senior adult will deal with sorrows, pain, and losses. Some of the losses senior adults experience include the loss of:

- Spouse
- Close friends
- Family members
- Health and stamina
- Physical mobility
- Finances
- Control over circumstances
- Dreams and goals
- Respect and status

Some of these losses, such as the loss of a lifelong mate, are very tangible, and they stab like a knife. Other losses are more abstract, such as the realization "I'll never be twenty-one again, I'll never be able to travel like I wanted, I'll never realize my ambitions." Whether tangible or intangible, these losses must be grieved in order to be resolved in a healthy way. One of the ways we can truly love and honor our parents as they move into the final years of life is by helping them to go through the process of grieving their losses. Let's examine what loss is like from a senior adult's point of view.

THE GRIEF PROCESS

"When my mother died after a long battle with cancer," Frank recalls, "I was amazed at how well my father handled it. He grieved. He cried. He went through the whole process, and after a few months he seemed to be coming back, getting into his old activities, developing some new hobbies, and really starting to enjoy life again.

"But about five months after Mom died, my dad's old Army buddy, Pete, a guy my dad had known for fifty years, collapsed and died of a heart attack. Dad took it really hard. I mean, he went into a tailspin. Complete depression. Couldn't eat, couldn't sleep. He just sat around the house and stared and talked about death.

"My dad always had a real strong faith in God when I was growing up. When Mom died, he talked about how happy she must be with Jesus in heaven. But when Pete died, he kept saying things like, 'How could a loving God take away a guy like Pete? He was the best friend a guy ever had, and he had plenty of years ahead of him.' Dad really blamed God for Pete's heart attack.

"It's hard to figure out," Frank concludes, "why these two losses—the loss of a life mate and the loss of a close friend—affected my Dad so differently."

Different losses can affect our senior adult parents in different and sometimes surprising ways. Normally, the loss of a spouse, particularly if one has been married many years, will have a greater and more devastating emotional impact than the loss of a close friend. But there are other factors which make up a loss besides the closeness of the relationship.

For example, the *circumstances of the loss* can be a factor. In terms of the closeness of a relationship, Frank's father was certainly closer to his wife than to his old army buddy. But these two important people in the life of Frank's father died under very different circumstances. His wife died after a lingering, painful illness. When she died, there was a sense of loss but also a sense of relief: "She's in heaven now and out of her suffering." But when Pete died, the loss was sudden and unexpected, and it seemed unfair. Instead of relief, Frank's father felt anger at the seeming unfairness of Pete's death.

Another factor which can compound a loss is the *timing of the loss*. Pete died only five months after Frank's mother died, at a time when Frank's father was just recovering from the previous loss. When too many losses come into a person's life close together, they can overwhelm a person. One's perception of life easily becomes distorted. After one loss, a person might respond (after grieving and gaining some perspective), "That was a very painful event, but life is essentially good, and I will get on with enjoying my life." But if two or three or four losses come close together, that person's outlook on life may become "Life is a painful experience, filled with catastrophes. Life is unfair, and it's too hard for me to deal with."

One more factor which affects the way people experience loss is the *general stability of one's life*. If your parent is working under the pressure of trying to keep a struggling business going, plus worrying about your brother who is going through a divorce, plus serving on the church board as the church is going through a time of intense conflict and division, and *then* a significant loss occurs, that loss is going to have a much more devastating impact than if the loss were to occur during a relatively stress-free period of his life. Experiencing a major loss during a time of significant stress is like riding a unicycle across a tightrope while juggling pineapples—and *then* getting beaned in the head by a hardball!

As you watch your senior adult parent going through a time of loss, you will be better able to understand what she is going through if you can place that experience within the larger context of her life: How closely is this loss tied to your parent's sense of well-being and personhood? Does your parent feel that most of her life has just been ripped away, or does your parent see this as a painful but recoverable situation? Have many losses, great or small, been clustering in your parent's life lately? Did this loss come at an already stressful period in her life?

The next factor to understand is the grief process itself. For most people, a major loss precipitates a grief process that follows a fairly predictable pattern. The five stages of grief were first recognized and made famous by Swiss psychiatrist Elisabeth Kubler-Ross in her 1969 book, *On Death and Dying.* Those stages are:

- Denial (or Shock): "This can't be happening to me!"
- Anger: "This is unfair!"
- Bargaining (or Magical Thinking): If the person faces an impending loss, he bargains, "Please, God, I'll do anything if you just keep this loss from happening." If the loss has already happened (such as the loss of a loved one), bargaining might take this form: "Please, God, I'll do anything if you'll take this pain away!" For people who have no belief in a personal God, bargaining may take the form of magical thinking: "If I do this good deed, think that good thought, get touched by a magical healer, or take some magic pill, everything will be all right."
- Despair: "This is the way it is, and it is unbearable."
- Acceptance: "This is the way it is, and I will accept it and do the best I can to get on with my life."

You can usually observe a grief process very much like this one in the experience of *any* significant loss—a financial loss, the loss of one's own health, the illness or death of a loved one, the loss of a marriage due to divorce, or the approaching loss of one's own life. In senior adults, however, it is not uncommon to see this entire grief process take a very compressed form, and the stages of the process are less clearly defined. Often, an older person will suffer a devastating loss and go right to the fourth stage—despair—and get stuck there. A person who is stuck in despair is a likely candidate for severe depression.

This does not mean you should expect your grieving parent to bounce back and be happy after some arbitrary number of weeks or months of grieving. One of the worst things people sometimes do when a loved one is grieving is to say, "Snap out of it! Be happy that your spouse is in heaven!" No, a parent needs to grieve her losses, and it can be very harmful if people try to rush or short-circuit that process. Grieving people need to cry. They need to mourn. They need to *feel* all the emotions of the grief process or they may never get beyond those emotions.

In some cases—for example, the loss of a mate after a long, successful marriage—it may be quite normal for a person to experience sadness, longing, and even crying from time to time for the rest of his life. It would not be realistic to expect such a deep loss to ever be completely grieved, in the sense that all sadness completely disappears. So it is possible for a person to be emotionally well-adjusted and healthy, yet frequently sad because a beloved mate is gone. Long-term sadness should not be confused with clinical depression.

In a healthy process of grieving, a person will generally be able to go through the stages of grief—shock, anger, bargaining, and despair—then emerge into a place of acceptance. That person will then be able to get on with her life. This doesn't mean that the five stages will be clear-cut. You won't say, "On Tuesday, Mom finished her anger and started her bargaining." Sometimes these stages get a little blurry and a person may actually backtrack, feeling anger in the midst of despair or falling back into denial for a few days after reaching a place of acceptance. Remember, these stages are a general description of a process that takes place in a very personal and highly individual way in each human being.

You may not see your parent express denial, anger, or bargaining. Instead, you may see your parent plunge immediately into deep sadness and despair. You should not be alarmed if your parent goes into such a state following a major loss. This does not mean that your parent is short-circuiting the grief process. You don't need to say to your parent, "Hey! Where's your denial? Where's your anger? Where's your bargaining? Go back and do it right!" Be aware that some of the grief stages may not be outwardly visible.

When a person suffers a major loss, it is normal to feel that just going on, day by day, is a challenge beyond endurance. The first few weeks after a loss are the hardest and most stressful weeks that a person will ever have to endure. The fact that our parents struggle with anger and sadness and a desire to withdraw from life does not mean they are psychologically malfunctioning. It just means they are human.

However, we also need to be aware that this is a crucial time in our parent's life. Here are some practical suggestions to help you encourage your parent to continue moving toward a successful resolution of the grief process:

Encourage your parent to talk openly and frankly about the lost loved one and about her feelings. Invite your parent to share memories—happy, unhappy, or bittersweet.

Listen nonjudgmentally. Encourage honesty and avoid showing disapproval of anything your parent says. Grieving people need to express the full range of their experience with that lost loved one, both the good memories and the bad. Doing so will help them get in touch with emotions they may have pushed aside for years.

Be especially aware of a parent who suffers in silence. Men especially tend to be good at "stuffing" their emotions, burying and denying their feelings in an unhealthy way. Encourage your grieving father to express his feelings. Let him know it is okay for a man to cry and to talk about his pain.

Encourage your parent to maintain daily routines of self-care, healthy functioning, and involvement with life: spending time with friends, participation in favorite activities (clubs, churches, social activities), maintaining personal hygiene (regular eating habits, bathing, grooming, and brushing teeth), spiritual disciplines and pastimes (Bible reading, fellowship, prayer, listening to Christian music). If months go by and your parent does not reconnect with these routines and interests, then professional help may be indicated.

Encourage your parent to plug into a support system. Many churches offer grief classes and support groups, often with a special focus on senior adults. If you can't locate such a support system through a church in your area, contact a professional counselor for help in finding a grief recovery class or support group.

Encourage your parent to express his feelings in writing. He might keep a journal or record feelings and experiences in letters to trusted friends. You might even encourage your parent to write a letter to God or to the lost loved one, expressing honest feelings about the loss that he might not feel comfortable saying to another person.

You should be aware that in some cases the despair and sadness can harden into true clinical depressions. So for the first few months after a major loss, be attentive to your parent's emotional state.

How do you know if your parent's grief has gone beyond healthy mourning to become clinical depression, requiring professional help? The most important warning sign is a *lack of progress* in dealing with the loss. In the case of a significant loss, such as the loss of a spouse, your parent may grieve for a long time—even one, two, three years or more. A long period of grief is not necessarily unhealthy. But you should expect to see *month-by-month progress* in your parent's emotions and relationships during that time. As weeks and months pass, you should see your parent begin to resume friendships, hobbies, and important activities. If, after a few months, your parent is still as immobilized, debilitated, and isolated as during the first few weeks or if he actually seems to be getting *more* withdrawn and nonfunctional, then your parent may be clinically depressed.

True clinical depression is a condition which requires treatment by a professional psychologist or psychiatrist. A person experiencing acute depression will show some or all of these symptoms:

- Sleeping disorders (either an inability to get to sleep, sleep that is frequently interrupted, or staying in bed all day)
- Long-term loss of appetite
- Emotions of either sadness or anger that last longer than three or four months
- Long-term loss of interest in once pleasurable activities (gardening or other hobbies, recreational pursuits, social pursuits, church or club activities, and so forth)
- Lack of attention to personal hygiene and grooming
- Sitting alone and staring
- Frequent crying spells

If you believe your parent is suffering from clinical depression, talk to her about seeing a counselor or a physician. Emphasize that if she is clinically depressed, she won't be able to just "snap out of it," nor can she depend on time to make it better. Clinical depression is a medical condition that must be treated.

DEALING WITH CONFLICTING EMOTIONS

Many senior adults seem to have conflicting emotions in the aftermath of a loss. They may say things which their adult children find troubling or even offensive. Alicia, for example, reports that she was absolutely horrified by her father's comments the day after her mother died. She explains, "Dad told me, 'It's a relief your mother is gone. That woman just tied me down.' Then a few hours later, he was crying and saying, 'How am I going to live without her?' Is he going crazy or what?"

No, Alicia's father is not going crazy. He is trying to make sense of what is right now an incomprehensible loss. Each of us is a collection of ambivalent and conflicting emotions. One of the classic emotional issues we all face is what psychologists call the *approach-avoidance conflict*. When someone causes us pain, we try to avoid that person. But when the pain is gone, we miss the pleasing aspects of that person and we want to approach that person again. During a time of loss and grief, our emotions may swirl from approach to avoidance and back again, over and over.

Another form of emotional conflict you may see in a grieving parent is that which results when your parent's mate dies after a lingering and painful illness such as cancer. Your parent may wobble back and forth between relief: "I'm so glad he's out of his pain, and that he's in heaven with Jesus" to grief: "I don't know how I can go on without him!" Your parent may even express what sound like very selfish feelings of relief: "It was so hard taking care of him every day while he was dying. At least now I can get some rest." Those are valid feelings. It doesn't mean your parent didn't love her spouse; it just means that life has been very hard and stressful. Help your parent to not feel guilty for such feelings. She should be encouraged to express those feelings as well as to grieve the loss of her mate.

After a major loss, there will probably be at least one well-meaning but misguided person who will approach your parent and, referring to 1 Thessalonians 4:13, say, "Hey, don't cry! Be happy that your mate has gone to be with the Lord! Remember, the Good Book says that we shouldn't grieve!" If someone says that to your parent, then help your parent to understand that this person has twisted the meaning of that passage. First Thessalonians 4:13 doesn't say that Christians shouldn't grieve, it says that we shouldn't grieve as those who have no hope! The only honest, healthy response to a major loss is *grief*. Pretending that a loss isn't really a loss is a sure way to produce emotional, psychological, and even physical disorders.

There is great practical wisdom in the words of Jesus from the Beatitudes: "Blessed are those who mourn, for they shall be comforted.[1] Those who mourn find peace and wholeness and comfort. Those who do not adequately mourn their losses may never get beyond their grief. They may even get mired in depression. To paraphrase the words of Jesus, tragic and unfortunate are those who are not allowed to mourn, for they shall never be comforted.

When Gladys lost her seventy-two-year-old husband, Ernie, she didn't want his funeral to be comprised of the standard glowing tributes that characterized most funerals. "At this funeral," she said, "we are going to tell the truth about Ernie." When Gladys told her daughter Lea about her plans for Ernie's funeral, Lea tried to talk her out of it, but Gladys would not be dissuaded. "Lea," said Gladys, "your father was an honest, plain-talking man, and this is going to be an honest, plain-talking funeral."

The funeral opened in the usual way, with organ music and a soloist, a preacher, and a eulogy. Then Gladys stood and said, "We're going to do something a little different at this last service for my husband, Ernie. There are some thoughts I want to share about Ernie, and after I've had my say, feel free to get up and say whatever's on your mind.

"To begin with, my late husband hurt a lot of people. He could be a mean-tempered, self-centered old curmudgeon. Ernie never meant to hurt anyone. Being blunt as a hammer was just his way. Some of the people in this room have felt the sandpaper side of Ernie's tongue, so you know exactly what I mean. I have to be honest with you. I'm not going to miss that side of my husband's personality. He and I argued many times in our fifty-one years of married life, and there were many times I cried my eyes out over that stubborn old man."

Gladys paused, inhaled a ragged breath, and looked around the chapel. The room was completely silent. Her voice shook as she continued. "But I *will* miss this about Ernie: his love for children and young people, his love for nature, his love for God. That feisty old man changed a lot of lives and led a lot of young people to Jesus Christ. And you know, the same nasty trait that made him so hard to live with was also the virtue that made him such a saint: Ernie was never afraid to tell you exactly what was on his mind. That made him as fearless as the apostle Paul. Because what was most on his mind was how much he wanted everyone to know his friend Jesus. I'd like to think that when we leave this place, we'll all take a little of Ernie's courage and honesty with us."

After Gladys sat down, others stood and shared stories and memories of Ernie—of both Ernie the saint and Ernie the "tough old bird." Everyone agreed that it was exactly the kind of memorial Ernie himself would have wanted and that it was the most meaningful funeral they had ever attended. Even though Lea was originally horrified by the idea, her mother had found a way to make sense of the conflicting emotions she felt after the loss of her husband. Afterwards, Lea agreed that it was good for Gladys, for Lea, and for everyone at the service to honestly admit their ambivalent feelings for her father.

Senior adults should always be encouraged to express, not repress, their honest feelings after a loss, even if those feelings are filled with uncomfortable contradictions.

WHAT TO DO WITH A DEPRESSED PARENT

Ellie's mother, Jane, was a problem. She had been a problem as long as Ellie could remember. Throughout Ellie's childhood, Jane had been a bitter, angry, verbally abusive, and sometimes physically abusive mother. Jane had married three times and divorced three times, and all three husbands had been abusive men. Since her last divorce, ten years earlier, Jane had lived the life of a recluse, a virtual hermit. For reasons that her daughter Ellie could never fully understand, Jane felt victimized by the world. She had no friends, no activities; she had only her TV, her bitterness, her worsening health, and her deepening depression. Various neighbors, churches, and social agencies offered assistance to Jane. There were offers to clean up her weed-infested yard and paint her dingy house, offers of free counseling and free medical care, but she turned them all down.

In time, Jane's health deteriorated to a point where she came to Ellie and said, "I need you to come live with me and take care of me."

"But I can't do that," said Ellie. "I've got a husband and two kids who need me."

"You've got a mother who needs you," Jane shot back. "Husbands come and go and kids take care of themselves, but you've only got one mother."

"My husband doesn't come and go," Ellie replied, "and my kids don't take care of themselves. They only have one mother too."

Jane turned and walked away. "The whole world has walked all over me," she grumbled bitterly. "Why should my own ungrateful daughter be any different?"

Ellie knew she couldn't just drop her husband and children and go live with her mother twenty-four hours a day, but she didn't know how to respond to her. Jane had Ellie so twisted up with guilt she felt like a pretzel inside. When she came to me, Ellie was a bundle of confused, raw emotions. She felt sorry, guilty, and responsible for Jane, but she was also angry with her mother almost to the point of hatred.

"She won't listen to me," said Ellie. "Nothing I say gets through to her. She doesn't care that I have a family and responsibilities. It doesn't occur to her that if she had taken some of the help that people have offered her, she wouldn't need to lean on me this way."

I asked Ellie if she knew why her mother was so depressed and withdrawn. "No," said Ellie, "she never talks about her past or why she is the way she is. She just complains about how unfair life is and how terrible people are." I suggested to

Ellie that she do some research to find out more about her mother's history. That week, Ellie called her Aunt Flo, Jane's sister, and talked to her about Jane's problems. Flo told Ellie some things she had never heard before—about how Jane and Flo and their siblings had been physically and verbally abused by their father in childhood and about other experiences in Jane's life that had embittered her and tilted her toward depression. Ellie was able to understand her mother better after that conversation, but it didn't change the fact that Jane was still fully responsible for her own life and her own feelings. Ellie tried to talk to Jane about her emotional issues, but Jane refused. Then Ellie encouraged Jane to seek counseling. Again, Jane refused. All Jane wanted was for Ellie to leave her family, come live with her, and take care of her twenty-four hours a day.

The next time Ellie and I talked, one thing was clear: nothing Ellie did was going to "work" in the sense that she could do this or say that and the problem would be solved. If Jane was depressed and nonfunctioning, then only Jame could take the steps to solve the problem. Ellie couldn't do it for her. But Ellie *could* confront Jane with the choices she should make.

So I suggested that Ellie write a letter to her mother. Letters can be valuable tools in situations where communication easily gets tangled and confused. In a letter, you can think through what you want to say, you can edit, you can get your message across without interruptions, and you can refer to a copy of the letter after you send it if need be. So Ellie wrote to her mother a brief three-paragraph letter. (In most cases, the shorter the letter, the clearer the communication.) Her essential message was:

> Mother, I love you, and I want the best for you.
> You need help—medical, psychological, and social help. Various people and agencies have offered you that help and you have turned it down. You need to accept

their help, because I cannot help you, and I will not help you.

I hope you realize that I truly do love you, even though I cannot help you.

Jane never did get help. Even though it tore Ellie up inside to refuse her mother's demands, she couldn't do anything else and still be faithful to her responsibilities to her family. Ellie was not responsible to do for her mother what her mother refused to do for herself.

"I WANT TO DIE"

John's eighty-two-year-old father, Harvey, was diagnosed with prostate cancer. The doctors assured Harvey that it is a slow growing cancer that can easily be controlled. "To Dad," said John, "the word 'cancer' is a death sentence. He's gone into a deep depression. He won't eat. He won't talk to anybody. And he's aging right before our eyes. The doctors say he could have at least another five years on this earth if he wanted it but that his emotional state could kill him long before the cancer would. I just don't know what to do to pull Dad out of this funk."

Dara's mother, Jennie, had no physical problems that the doctors could find, but ever since her husband died a year before, she was losing weight, aging visibly, and generally withdrawing from life. "She was always a social butterfly," said Dara. "But now she sits in her bedroom with the shades pulled. She won't see visitors. When I come to see her, I have to let myself in with my key because she won't answer the door. She won't answer the phone. She says things like, 'I'm just in the way,' or, 'I just wish I could die.' I'm afraid she's going to waste away—or that she might even take her own life. I don't know what to do with her."

Both John and Dara have reason to be concerned for their parents. For many people, particularly for the elderly, depression can be a life-threatening illness. Research shows that when a person loses a mate after a long marriage, that person's chances of dying within a few months to a year increase dramatically. The reasons are not hard to find: traumatic grief usually degrades a person's will to live, and when the mind says, "I don't want to live," the body frequently cooperates with the mind and says, "Very well, let's just shut down."

The body of a grieving person tends to produce fewer antibodies to fight infection and cancer. The stressful emotions of grief also affect the functioning of the hypothalamus (the portion of the brain that regulates appetite, sleep patterns, body temperature, emotions, and other vital functions), the pituitary gland (which regulates the activity of other glands, such as the thyroid gland), and the adrenal glands (which secrete stress hormones).

If you are dealing with a depressed parent, here are some actions you can take to help your parent's mental and emotional state:

Encourage your depressed parent to undergo a full medical evaluation. There are a lot of of factors that contribute to clinical depression, including depletion or imbalance of certain chemicals in the brain or other physical problems. These biochemical deficiencies can occur because of emotional stress, poor diet, vitamin deficiency, medication (including certain tranquilizers and high blood pressure medications), or glandular malfunction. A geriatric specialist or psychiatrist can often diagnose and treat organic malfunctions which affect a person's emotional state.

Encourage your senior parent to seek counseling. Help him to understand that it is a sign of strength and courage, not weakness, to obtain counseling. Many people from your parents' generation feel there is a stigma attached to getting professional psychological help. They need to hear from you that they do not have to suffer. Their depression can be treated and alleviated.

Offer to give the physician, psychiatrist, or counselor your perspective on your parent's emotional problems. Family members can often provide perspective and details that the patient might not recall or think important. For example, you might tell the doctor, "Mom sometimes says, 'I wish the Lord would just take me.'" That information can be an important clue to the doctor—and one which your parent might never share.

Affirm your parent not only for what she does but just for the irreplaceable unique person she is. Our culture tends to stress that people are valued for what they offer or for what they accomplish. Consequently, as people age and lose their ability to work and be productive, they often begin to feel they have nothing to offer and are no longer valued. They become physically debilitated, life becomes more difficult and more painful, they suffer more and deeper losses in life, and they may even be robbed of the capacity to see, hear, or communicate well. Soon, distorted thinking sets in, and they begin to think they would be better off dead. This kind of thinking makes them more susceptible to fatal illness or suicide.

Let your senior parent know that you value time spent with him, hearing his voice, sharing stories and memories, and continuing a relationship that has been important to you throughout your life. Let your parent know that you treasure his prayers. Reassure your parent that he is significant.

When your depressed parent says, "I want to die," help her to see her life in spiritual terms. For example, you might say, "When God is ready and you are ready, He will call you home. But you are alive now, so God must have a good reason for keeping you here."

Affirm to your parent that he is loved and needed. Depression is often complicated by *distorted thinking*, a skewed and unrealistic evaluation of one's circumstances. One example of distorted thinking occurs when people become suicidal and think to themselves, "My spouse and my children would be better off without me," when in fact a realistic evaluation would tell this person that suicide is the most devastating and hurtful act one can commit against one's own family.

Another example of distorted thinking occurs when senior adults say to themselves, "I'm worthless. I'm in the way. I'm just a burden to everyone. No one wants me around." One service we can do for our senior parents when they fall into distorted thinking is to reassure them of their meaning and importance in our lives and of the fact that they continue to be a blessing by their mere presence with us.

If you believe your parent is planning suicide, take positive action. Here is a step-by-step plan for suicide intervention:

- If your parent mentions suicidal feelings, don't ignore or deny those feelings. Talk about them frankly and calmly. Don't be afraid that you are giving your parent ideas by discussing the subject of suicide. If she has already said things like "I wish I were dead," then the idea is already there. Don't leave your parent alone with those thoughts. Remember: depression distorts thinking and emotions. Help your parent sort through those feelings and thoughts and find a more realistic perspective.
- Listen nonjudgmentally. Avoid expressing shock, anger, or dismay. Don't be quick to speak. Avoid dogmatic statements such as "Suicide is a sin," or "People who kill themselves go to hell." Express empathy and understanding.
- Act on the assumption that your parent is seriously intent on committing suicide. Don't say, "You aren't serious," or dare your parent, "Go ahead and do it."
- If possible, remove the means of suicide from your parent's reach. Don't leave your parent alone. Don't give him the opportunity to carry out a suicide plan.
- Contact a crisis intervention or suicide prevention

agency *immediately*. Your parent needs professional
evaluation, and may require inpatient care in order
to get past this crisis.

If you prevent a planned suicide, your parent may scream,
cry, or threaten you. Reassure yourself that you are doing the
right thing. If your parent is angry with you now, it is because
she is operating with distorted thinking. Once your parent's
distorted thinking has been corrected and some of the emotional and chemical factors contributing to the depression
have been resolved, your parent will probably be grateful to
you and say, "I don't know what got into me. I see now how
wrong it was to want to kill myself, but I just couldn't see it
then."

Recognize and accept the limits of your own responsibility.
If your parent dies, even if your parent commits suicide, *it is
not your fault*. You are not responsible for what your parent
does. Everyone must take responsibility for his own life. If
your parent chooses not to seek help, or not to change, or not
to get better, or even not to live, that is your parent's choice,
and you are not to blame.

AGING, ILLNESS, AND PERSONALITY CHANGE

"Within a few weeks after my mother passed away," says
Brock, "my father just went off the deep end. His behavior
became really—well, I don't want to call it crazy, but it certainly is bizarre. Sometimes Dad talks about Mom as if she's
still alive, and sometimes he cries uncontrollably because
she's gone.

"He was always so even-tempered and polite, but now he
gets angry at the drop of a hat, and he'll swear at you or tell
you to shut up—things I *never* heard him say before. He's actually accused me and my sister of spying on him!

"His judgment seems really impaired. He buys things he
can't possibly use, and he gives away mementos and keep-

sakes that he and Mom treasured for years. His mood bounces from pole to pole without warning. One moment he's joking with you and laughing, and the next moment he's screaming at you and looking like he could happily slit your throat!

"Recently, I found out that Dad's been bleeding from the bowels for several weeks, but he refuses to go to a doctor and have it checked out. I just don't know what to do about him."

Unfortunately, personality changes and irrational behavior sometimes accompany the grief of a major loss such as Brock's father experienced. In addition, mood disorders are a common component of aging, and we may not always be able to single out one event or cause or catalyst for these problems.

One factor in personality changes is that humans lose brain cells as they get older. The average person has all the brain cells he will ever have by age six months. In other words, in terms of brain capacity, we are all over the hill six months after we are born! By age sixty-five, the average person has only 75 percent of the 10 billion brain cells he had at age six months. This doesn't mean your senior adult parent is doomed to mental deterioration—after all, that sixty-five-year-old senior still has a respectable 7 or 8 billion brain cells left! But it does mean that, for most older people, certain mental functions—thinking, focusing, analyzing, memorizing, and remembering—may not come as easily as they used to. Behavior may become more selfish, childish, extreme, and socially unacceptable as the inhibitory centers of the brain (which help us control our behavior, our emotions, and our appetites) begin to weaken. Reaction time may be slowed. Judgment may be impaired.

Aging and the stress of loss, grief, and anger can affect the levels of certain important chemicals in the brain. These chemicals, called *neurotransmitters*, include such substances as serotonin and dopamine, which have a powerful impact on the way we feel and think. When serotonin levels in the brain dip too low, the result is a decrease in the ability to concentrate and remember and an increased tendency toward irritability and depression. When dopamine becomes too active in the brain, the result can be delusions (irrational beliefs), visual and auditory hallucinations (seeing things that aren't there or hearing nonexistent sounds and voices), and paranoia (believing that one is being watched, followed, attacked, or conspired against).

Of course, symptoms such as memory loss, confusion, slurred speech, and personality changes can also be symptoms of Alzheimer's disease. As yet, there is no known cure or prevention for Alzheimer's, and the causes of the disease have not yet been determined. Some studies indicate that there may be some link between Alzheimer's disease and one or more of the following conditions:

- Abnormally high concentrations of aluminum in the brain
- A deficiency in the neurotransmitter acetylcholine
- Gene mutation, resulting in abnormally high concentrations of a substance called beta-amyloid

Although there is presently no cure for Alzheimer's disease, there are treatments available which can alleviate the symptoms of the disease. Consult your geriatric specialist for more information.

Very often, older people will show signs of confusion, forgetfulness, or other unusual behavior, and their loved ones will too hastily chalk it up to old age. In many cases, these symptoms are in fact the treatable and reversible effects of depression or some other temporary disorder. Any senior adult who shows such symptoms should be medically evaluated. The quality of a senior adult's life can often be dramatically improved along with her ability to concentrate, remember, think, and sleep.

If, like Brock, you have a parent who needs help but refuses to see a professional counselor, psychiatrist, or physician, there are steps you can take to lovingly persuade your parent to be evaluated and treated. If your parent's behavior is particularly extreme or difficult to deal with, consider involving a professional counselor in the process. Here is a suggested strategy:

Discuss the problem with three or four other close family members who love your parent and whom he trusts. Choose people who are wise and mature and who can be counted on to prayerfully love your parent, even in a difficult situation. Make sure that everyone in that group understands the problem and is on board and in agreement with you in solving that problem.

Bring those family members together with your parent. This gathering is called an *intervention.* As a group, express your love to your parent and tell him, "Because we want the best for you, we are going to take you right now to see a doctor so that you can get well."

If your parent still refuses to see a doctor, don't use force. Instead, contact an attorney and go through the process of legal commitment through the courts.

Be prepared for crying, anger, and threats. Continue to reassure your parent of your love for him throughout the process. Once treatment begins, the symptoms usually subside. In time, your parent will probably be grateful that you have taken this difficult but loving step to help him get better.

But even if your parent is never grateful or has a condition which does not improve, you have lost nothing. If your parent is undergoing such an intense and painful disorder, you have to *try* to get your parent into treatment. You must determine, firmly and irrevocably, that your parent *will* get the help she needs.

If your parent requires medical attention or hospitalization, here are some ways you can make sure she gets the best care and attention:

Be available to your parent to help her sort through medical options and make decisions. Accompany your parent on visits to the doctor and be assertive in asking questions she may not think to ask. Listen carefully to the doctor's explanations and take notes. Your parent may not fully hear or grasp everything that the doctor says, and you can help your parent understand everything that is being done on her behalf.

Help your parent select doctors and hospitals which will understand their needs. Senior adults are often apprehensive about going into a hospital, wondering, "Will the medical staff understand what I'm going through? Will I be treated as a human being with feelings and a life to live or as an old person whose life is already behind me?" Your parent doesn't want to be treated as a set of symptoms; he wants to be seen as an individual.

Check with friends and with your pastor. Ask which doctors and hospitals have a reputation for dealing compassionately with the emotional and physical needs of older patients. Find out which facilities emphasize friendly, personal, understanding geriatric care.

If your parent is ever hospitalized, be assertive in making sure he is properly cared for. Even in the best and most conscientious facilities, personnel may sometimes overlook your parent's needs, due to overwork or a simple oversight. Be courteous and respectful but clear in communicating with hospital staff on your parent's behalf.

Make sure that your parent's spiritual needs are being met as well. Arrange for visitation by pastors, elders, or friends from your church or your parent's church. Ask for prayer from prayer groups in the church. Pray with your parent and don't hesitate to discuss spiritual issues with her. Ask your parent if she would like a Bible or Christian books to read or Christian tapes to listen to.

OUR HOME OR THE OLD FOLKS' HOME?

Brian chose the dinner hour to make his big announcement to the family. "Honey. Kids. Guess what?" he asked nervously. "Grandma's coming to live with us! Isn't that great?"

Brian's three children said nothing but looked stricken. His wife, Nancy, however, had *plenty* to say, but she waited until after the kids were in bed to say it.

"How could you?" she began.

"How could I what?"

"You know what, Brian. How could you invite your mother to come live with us and then waltz in and announce it to the family? No discussion, no input, no nothing! There are four other people in this family who should have a voice in such matters."

"The kids don't get a vote."

"I didn't say a vote. I said a voice. And you didn't let any of us say anything about this decision. Face it, Brian, your mother isn't the easiest person to . . . No, let's say it straight out. Your mother is a *pain in the neck!* She drives the kids crazy, she drives me crazy, she even drives *you* crazy!"

"Look, Nancy, in my family, we kids were raised to take care of our parents when they get old. Mom's in her seventies, she's getting frail, and she can't take care of herself. It's an obligation, and obligations are not open for discussion. She's living with us."

"I've got news for you, Brian! This is one obligation that's gonna get discussed—and how! For openers, I'm not letting that woman live in my house! Not now, not ever!"

The "discussion" escalated from there and ended two hours later without agreement. The "discussion" continued in my office. Brian continued to feel that his strong family obligation overrode any objections of his wife. Nancy, on the other hand, continued her absolute refusal.

As we sorted through the issues on both sides, we discovered that in this case (as in most cases of marital conflict), there were more issues involved than just the question of Brian's mother living in their house. Nancy's feelings were contaminated not only by an unpleasant history with her mother-in-law but also by appalling memories of the time her own grandmother came to live with her family when she was twelve years old. And it turned out that the reason Brian had taken the unprecedented step of making a major decision without discussing it with the family was that Brain felt Nancy didn't respect his opinion. Fearing he would lose the argument—or the "discussion"—he attempted to head off an argument by simply laying down the law.

After we worked out these "side-dish" issues, we then tackled the "main course": what to do about Brian's mom. We explored such questions as:

- What does it mean, in practical terms, to truly honor Brian's mother?
- What other alternatives are there to having Brian's mother live with Brian's family?
- What would be the best living arrangement for Brian's mother, in terms of her own real needs?
- What would be the best arrangement for Brian, Nancy, and the children?
- What is Brian's true obligation to his mother, and to his family?

From a Christian perspective, we *all* have an obligation to our aging parents. First Timothy 5:8 tells us, "If anyone does not provide for his own, and especially for those of his household, he has denied the faith and is worse than an unbeliever." If you examine that verse in context, you see that it is talking primarily about taking care of the elderly in your own household. This verse is telling us that we do not have the option to simply abandon our parents or put them on the shelf. Yes, we have our own lives to lead, but if we deny the lives of the people who raised us, we might as well deny our Christian faith.

So we have a clear biblical obligation to care for our senior adult parents. But does that mean that we *must* take our parents into our own home? Before making this decision, consider these questions:

- Would this move be best for my parent? Does my parent require care and a protective environment that I am not able to provide?
- Will I be able to maintain reasonable, healthy boundaries if my parent lives in my house?
- Will my spouse and I be able to resolve the usual marital and family conflicts with Mom or Dad around all the time?
- Is my parent abusive? manipulative? controlling? Will he soak up my time and emotional energy in a way that is not healthy for my parent, my family, or myself?

In general, experience shows that it is usually not a good idea for senior adult parents to live with their children on an extended basis. One of the principal reasons is *boundaries:* it is virtually impossible to have clear parent/adult-child boundaries while sharing the same four walls with that parent. Authority issues can become tangled ("This is my house, Dad!" "Well, it may be your house, but I'm your father!"). Old, unhealthy patterns of behaving and relating can reassert themselves.

Whether your parent is self-sufficient, totally dependent, or somewhere in between, she is likely to be better off living separate from you. A self-sufficient parent does not need continual live-in caretakers, just a visit and a phone call every now and then to make sure everything's all right. And a totally dependent senior adult requires more constant and professional care than you could reasonably supply.

For those senior adults who fall somewhere in between self-sufficiency and dependency—for example, a senior adult who is able to take care of most of his own needs but is at some risk due to diabetes, heart disease, arthritis, or some other physical problem—there are many living options available which didn't even exist twenty years ago. These options include living at home with a part-time or full-time private duty nurse or companion or living in a residential facility which provides apartment-style independence and privacy along with part-time nursing care (sometimes called "assisted living"). There are many such facilities which offer security, shops and food service, and immediate access to acute medical care. Some of these facilities require an up-front entrance fee or buy-in while others require only monthly rent.

Some living or convalescent care facilities will be better suited than others to the specific needs of your parent. Many nursing homes and intermediate care facilities offer a caring Christian environment for their residents. Ask friends who have loved ones in nursing homes which facilities they recommend. Research, interview, and tour various facilities, then present your findings to your parent in a way that makes the choices clear. Let him tour the facility before making a decision. If your parent is capable of making these decisions, avoid any appearance of trying to "railroad" him. As much as possible, help your parent to feel that he has a measure of control over such important life decisions.

If you and your parent decide that a nursing home would be the best option, there are specific actions you can take to make the transition easier and the quality of life better for him:

Ask your parent what keepsakes and mementos she would like to take to her new home. Perhaps photographs, reminders of grandchildren or of a spouse who passed away, treasured books, or a Bible would help your parent to have a sense that she is in a new home, not being shut up in an institution.

Give your parent a housewarming gift when he moves into the new surroundings. A plant, a framed picture, or some other homey object. Throw an intimate housewarming party with a few friends or family members. Put up streamers and balloons. Make this move feel like a festive occasion rather than a prison sentence.

As much as possible, involve your parent in decisions and

keep her informed about circumstances, options, doctors' advice, and so forth. Consider your parent's wishes. Many adult children dictate to their parents, manipulate their decisions, and shield them from information. When a senior adult feels he no longer has any control, input, or understanding regarding major life-changing decisions, that senior adult becomes a prime candidate for resentment and depression and can easily lose the will to live. Communicate to your parent that, despite this change of address, he still has a loving family and many more years of life to enjoy.

If your parent is ambulatory, make a regular habit (say, once or twice a month) of taking her out of the facility. Go to lunch, visit friends and relatives, have her hair done, go shopping, or just walk in the park. Be aware not only of your senior adult parent's limitations but also of her remaining capacity for mobility, activity, and enjoyment of activity.

Minister to your parent's spiritual needs. Get family members together for a "sing-along" at the nursing home. Take Mom or Dad out to the common room where the piano is and have a great time. Even seniors with advanced senility will often respond to familiar songs. You may be surprised to see a parent who hasn't responded to any other stimulus suddenly begin to clap or smile or sing along when he hears old favorites like "How Great Thou Art" and "Amazing Grace."

WHAT DO YOU DO WITH THE GUILT?

Colleen's father had lived with her and her husband for over ten years, ever since his first heart attack. A year ago, he was diagnosed with Alzheimer's disease. Against the advice of many people, including her father's doctor, she decided to keep her father at home and care for him.

But then her father, who was prone to getting up and wandering around the house at night, fell and broke his hip. At that point, Colleen had to face the fact that she could no longer care for her father at home. "I never thought I would ever place my father in a nursing home," she says, "but I realize now that I just can't take care of him at home. I visited the Alzheimer's Living Center, which is specially designed to give Alzheimer's patients a homelike environment. I could tell the patients were well cared for there, and the whole facility was designed to be as safe as possible for someone like Dad. There was a lot less likelihood that he would injure himself again like he did at home. But even though I know that the Living Center is really the best place for Dad, I still have a lot of guilt."

In counseling, I encouraged Colleen to examine the sources of the guilt she felt about putting her father in a clean, safe, caring facility specifically designed for her father's needs. Over two or three sessions, Colleen was able to discern several insights.

First, putting her father in a nursing home made Colleen feel that she had failed in her role as a caregiver and daughter. For the past ten years, a lot of Colleen's self-esteem was bound up in the fact that she was capable of caring for her father at home. She had often said, "I love my dad too much to put him in a home." After having prided herself on her love and caregiving for her father—and having practically boasted of this fact to family and friends—her sense of defeat in this area was a significant shame issue for her.

The move also stirred deep fears within Colleen; she was in her late fifties, and one of her greatest fears was the thought of having to be, as she put it, "shut up in an old folks' home."

Finally, Colleen had been raised with a misunderstanding of the biblical injunction given in 1 Timothy 5:8 to provide for those of our own household. She took that verse to mean that to be a good Christian, you must provide for your senior adult parents by taking them into your own home. This belief created a great load of misplaced religious guilt when she placed her father in a care facility.

Once these issues were out in the open, Colleen and I worked together on a plan to deal with her misplaced feelings of guilt and shame. Colleen set up a schedule of regular visits with her father at the Living Center. Her father was often disoriented, not knowing where he was or what year it was. On his worst days, he didn't even recognize Colleen, but most days he had enough clarity to appreciate her presence. By visiting her father on a regular pattern, Colleen helped her father—despite the debilitating effects of his illness—to discern a comfortable, stable pattern in his life.

Colleen also joined a support group for caregivers of Alzheimer's Patients. Though her church was too small to offer such groups, she located a large church nearby which offered dozens of support groups designed to meet a wide variety of needs.

Colleen continued in counseling for several months, working on the sources of her guilt and her compulsive need to rescue others. In counseling, she learned to better understand thy dynamics of guilt, compulsion, and lack of boundaries that led her to keep her father at home when it was not in his best interests or hers; and she discovered that some of these dynamics also played an unhealthy role in her relationship with her husband and her adult children.

Colleen decided that the one thing she could give her father that no one else could provide was her love. She made a decision that no matter what the state of his mental faculties might be, even on days when her father didn't recognize her, she would do everything possible to convey her love to him. "I talk to him, I stroke his hand, I call him Daddy, I read the Bible to him," she says. "I don't know how much of that gets through to him, but you never know."

Tim's mother lived in his home for six years. For most of that time, there were few problems, and it seemed to be an ideal arrangement. Mom had her own room on the far side of the family room, away from the other bedrooms, so there was a degree of boundary space even though she lived under the same roof with Tim and his family. But as his mother got older, Tim began to worry about her increasing dizzy spells, her osteoporosis, and the fact that sudden vertigo and brittle bones could be a deadly combination. There were times when she had to be left alone for the better part of a day, and Tim dreaded coming home some evening to find that his mother had been lying on the floor since morning. So he had a frank and caring talk with his mother, and they both agreed it would be better if she moved to a facility where she could have constant care and attention.

But that didn't end the matter. Some of Tim's Christian friends pelted him with Bible verses and advice, trying to convince him he was making a mistake. Tim's brother and sister called him from their homes in Texas and Illinois to chew him out for "tossing Mom into an institution." Fortunately, Tim was secure enough to know that he had made the right decision—and so had Mom.

"Look," he told his siblings, "I didn't throw Mom out of my house. I talked this decision over with her, and she thought it was a good idea too. If you can give Mom twenty-four hour care in your own home, then God bless you, I'll fly her out and deliver her to your door. But I can't give her that kind of care. Frankly, I'm not willing to come home some day and find Mom dead on the floor. I'd kind of like to keep her around for a while. I'd encourage you to get on a plane and visit Mom in her new home. I think you'll feel a lot better about it once you've seen the place."

No matter what decision you make, there will be those who tell you, "You're making a big mistake." When that happens, I encourage you to persevere. Do what you know is right. The loving thing to do is often the hardest thing to do. If you make decisions based on what is wise and loving rather than yielding to pressure, you will be able to look back five, ten, or twenty years from now and have no regrets.

IF YOUR PARENT LIVES WITH YOU

In some cases, the best thing for you and your parent may be to take your parent into your home. In some cases—particularly if your parent is a good example of spiritual and emotional health—it can be good for your children to have Grandma or Grandpa present as a character model and a spiritual influence. It can be very beneficial for your children to see you caring for your aging parent in tangible, practical ways. But before accepting such a responsibility, carefully consider the following points:

Remember that once you invite your parent into your home, you may find it difficult and awkward to "uninvite" her. The job can turn out to be bigger or more unpleasant than you can handle. This commitment is not to be entered into lightly.

Consider your family's need for boundaries and privacy. Before inviting your parent to live in your home, consider such options as establishing a "mother-in-law apartment" separate from your house or renting a house a few doors down from yours.

Be aware that giving care to a senior adult can be a very stressful and demanding full-time job. Research and experience both indicate that caregivers of elderly parents are much more susceptible than the general population to fatigue, depression, anxiety, ulcers, high blood pressure, and other stress-related disorders. Consider having a regular medical evaluation to make sure you are coping, emotionally and physically, with the demands of the job.

Be aware of your options. If you invite a needy, physically dependent parent into your home, you should be aware that many nursing homes offer "respite care" or "extended weekend care," which enables caregiving families to have a rest from their caregiving chores for a few days each week.

Consider joining a support group for caregivers of senior adults. Also, consider regular professional counseling to help you deal with the various stresses, decisions, and problems that will arise.

FOCUS FORWARD

No one enjoys simply existing. We all need a sense of meaning, of purpose, of progress in life. If we lose our ability to live forward-focused lives, we wither and die.

Perhaps the greatest challenge adult children face is encouraging and helping their parents to have a focus on the future. As our parent-child roles begin to reverse and we become caregivers to our parents, we have an opportunity to teach our parents truths that they may have never learned in life. Perhaps it is not too late for our parents to learn new skills and habits. Perhaps it is not too late for them to learn to disclose their feelings, to give and receive love. Perhaps it is not too late for them to receive the love of God, as it is expressed to them through our love.

The Bible says, "Even to your old age, I am He, and even to gray hairs I will carry you! . . . I will carry, and will deliver you."[2] Our God is a God who loves older people, people who have moved into the gray area of life. If he loves older people so much, then so should we.

As you love and care for these gray-haired people who once cared for you, you teach the next generation—your own children—that senior adults should be respected, honored, loved, and cared for. And you had better teach them well, because your day is coming.

But there is something even deeper taking place within you whenever you demonstrate love to your senior adult parents. As you serve and care for them, you can watch and learn what they are feeling and suffering. You can observe how they cope with the trial of growing old.

Your parents may not be saints. You may even bear scars—physical or emotional or both—from the way they have treated you as a child and as an adult. They may not be coping with old age very well because people who didn't cope well as young adults and middle-aged adults don't tend to suddenly blossom with character when they reach senior citizenship. And that should be a lesson to you and me. As we see the kind of character it takes to grow old, to experience loss after loss, to see the reins of life slipping from our hands, we would do well to build the kind of character and coping skills *now* that will serve us well when we are old.

Joni Eareckson Tada tells the story of how her husband Ken cared for his elderly father, who was physically and mentally disabled following a series of strokes. After three years of meeting his father's needs, giving him baths, and feeding him by hand, Ken became very tired and discouraged. One day, he came home and said, "Joni, I just don't understand why the Lord hasn't taken my father home. I'm just wondering if all this effort is really worth it."

The next day, Ken was again spending time with his father, feeding him lunch, when his father—who doesn't have many lucid moments—reached out and touched Ken's arm, looked at him straight in the eye, and said, "God likes you."

"What a shock!" Ken recounted to Joni that evening. "It really blew me away. It was as if Dad was personally hand-delivering a message from God to me."

What was that message? "It was a message," concludes Joni, "that God was pleased with my husband, Ken, for all the many months he had shown Christian care and compassion to his family. The Lord reaches over, touches your arm, looks you in the eye and says, 'I like you'"[3]

And that is God's word of encouragement to you, as you care for your senior adult parent: "The work you are doing is important. Keep it up. God likes you."

In the next chapter, we will take a closer look at our own parenting styles. We will answer the question many people ask who have been hurt or hindered by the parenting they have received: "How do I break the cycle? How do I keep from repeating the mistakes of my parents? How can I become the kind of parent I truly want to be?"

Breaking the Cycle

You want to brighten up that dingy corner of the family room, so you bring that old brass lamp down out of the attic, stand it in the corner, and—uh-oh. The bookcase is in front of the outlet. But if you move the bookcase, that sofa has to go someplace. And what do you do with that La-Z-Boy recliner? After you spend an hour and a half rearranging furniture, you are ready to plug in the lamp.

You insert the plug into the outlet, but nothing happens. The bulb must be burned out. So you get in the car, run down to Wal-Mart, and come back an hour later with two light bulbs and about a hundred dollars worth of other stuff you needed. You remove the lamp shade, stick a hundred-watter in the ol' socket, turn the switch, and—nothing. Then you remember why you put that old brass lamp in the attic in the first place: the power cord is broken under the base.

You remember buying a new cord way back when, intending to fix the lamp. Now where did you put that cord? You conduct a search of the garage. You move boxes, broken tricycles, and a lot of rusty gardening tools. You kill three black widows. You haul two loads of junk to the dump. And after five hours of cleaning, you find the cord in a paper bag, still with the original Reagan-era receipt, way back in the farthest, darkest recesses under the workbench.

You go back to the family room, install the new cord, plug it in, and that old brass lamp lights up brighter than the Christmas tree at Rockefeller Center! Mission accomplished—and the whole job took only ten hours!

Sometimes emotional and psychological problems are like that. You start with one problem, and soon you are dealing with interconnecting webs of relationships, old memories, recent hurts, and intergenerational cycles of pain, abuse, and enmeshment.

That was Deanna's situation when she came to my office for counseling, but she didn't realize it at the time. Deanna's "dingy corner"—that dark place in her emotional life where she wanted to plug in a lamp and find some light—was her relationship with her mother. Before she was finished working on this issue, however, she was going to have to rearrange the furniture of her relationships and clean out the garage of her memories.

"My mother always favored my sister over me," Deanna explained at the beginning of her first session. "I was an only child till I was twelve, then my sister Sara came along, 'a happy little accident,' my mother called her. I went from being the darling of the family to being treated like an outsider. Sara became the baby of the family, and even though she's thirty years old now, she's still the baby and I'm still an outsider.

"To this day, Sara can do no wrong, and I can do no right. Mom is always saying to me, 'Deanna, you used to be so pretty and now you're getting so fat! Why don't you take better care of yourself?' Or 'Deanna, that daughter of yours is practically growing up like a weed! If you didn't learn anything about being a parent from your father and me, you might at least take a few lessons from Sara!' Or 'Deanna, the way you keep house, it's no wonder your husband left you for another woman!' I know it's not right to feel this way, but I just wish I could cut my mother right out of my life!"

As we talked, it became clear that Deanna's problem with

her mother was bound up with so many other issues in her life that there was no way to attack this one issue in isolation. She had a serious weight problem, which was due to compulsive overeating, which in turn was due to unresolved anger and low self-esteem, which was due to her mother's verbal abuse and neglect in her adolescent years. She had a strained relationship with her sister Sara, the result of her mother's favoritism toward Sara and slighting of Deanna. There was considerable bitterness, guilt, shame, and self-hate in Deanna's life—the toxic residue of a very painful and humiliating divorce. And Deanna also had a very enmeshed relationship with her ten-year-old daughter, and that relationship was rooted in Deanna's own emotional impoverishment and loneliness.

Deanna's pain from her mother's verbal abuse was so great that she was almost blind to all the other issues in her life. The problem she was the *least* aware of was, in my view, the most urgent of all. Her ten-year-old daughter was at a very impressionable stage in life, and Deanna was laying down patterns of behaving and relating in her daughter's life that might impair her daughter's own emotional functioning and could even be passed down to succeeding generations.

So I confronted Deanna with the fact that she was caught up in a cycle—a truly vicious cycle—and that her most urgent need, if she really loved her daughter, was to *break* that cycle. At first, Deanna couldn't see that she had a problem with her daughter. After all, they had a great relationship—more like a friendship than a mother-daughter relationship. They spent a lot of time together. Her daughter didn't have any friends her own age, but she and Deanna were such good friends that it didn't really seem to matter. "It doesn't seem to be hurting her development any," Deanna reasoned. "After all, the kid has so much savvy, I find myself turning to her for advice more than she turns to me!"

What Deanna didn't realize was that everything that she cited as a positive dynamic in her relationship with her daughter was evidence of how enmeshed and overinvolved she was in her daughter's life. She was relying on her daughter for emotional support and counsel. In explaining the divorce to her daughter, Deanna had shared intimate facts, including sexual issues, about her troubled relationship with her ex-husband. "I even told her about those few months, right after my divorce," said Deanna, "when I felt depressed and suicidal. My daughter is really very mature, and she took it very well. She gave me a lot of support and encouragement." Deanna seemed to have no idea that a ten-year-old girl—no matter how mature she seems—is simply not equipped to cope with emotional issues of this magnitude.

Deanna was caught in a bind that many adult children of dysfunctional families find themselves in: they hate the things their parents did, yet they can't keep themselves from inflicting equally serious harm on their own children. Unhealthy family issues have an amazing ability to repeat themselves in cycles, generation after generation after generation. Unless you find some way to break that cycle, your own children are destined to suffer the same kinds of hurts you suffered in your own childhood.

THE CYCLE CAN BE BROKEN

In chapter 6, I stated that there are four ingredients that every child needs in order to have a happy and healthy life:

- A childhood of innocent joys, free of the pressures, trials, and responsibilities of adulthood
- A sense of control, accomplishment, and healthy self-direction in life
- Unconditional acceptance and validation of who he truly is
- Respect for her own feelings and thoughts

Unfortunately, not every child receives these basic minimum requirements, and you may have been one of those unfortunate children yourself. If so, then there is a significant risk that your own children, despite your best intentions and your love for them, may not be receiving those minimum requirements either.

In my own practice, I have observed that people from dysfunctional backgrounds tend to respond to their backgrounds by parenting their own children in one of two ways. They either adopt the parenting style and habits of their parents, or they react so rebelliously against that style that they over steer in the opposite but equally disastrous direction.

Those who copy the abusive, controlling, enmeshed, or neglectful parenting habits of their own parents may actually resent those traits in their parents, and they will tend to feel enormous guilt and self-hate when they realize they are doing the same kind of harm to their own children. But they lack the insights and the coping skills to stop themselves. They spent the most formative years of their lives being conditioned and taught that this is how parents behave. It is a monumental task to unlearn attitudes, habits, and conditioned responses that have been built up over nearly two decades of early life.

Those who respond to their parents' style by going to the other extreme often come to regret their own parenting style as much as they resented the approach of their parents. They promise themselves, "I will *never, ever, ever* be the kind of parent my Mom and Dad were." And in the process, they create a whole new set of problems in their children that they have no experience or skills in dealing with.

One of the first challenges I have as a counselor is getting people to see their own backgrounds with a little more objectivity and perspective. Many people coming into counseling already know that their childhood was "a little out of whack," but they never realized just how disordered their family truly was. They think all kids get punched and kicked and bruised all the time. Or they think it's normal to be told by your parents that you are stupid and ugly and you'll never amount to anything. Or they think it's normal to have been enmeshed and overprotected all your life.

Often as people are telling me their stories, I have to stop them and say, "Do you realize that what you are describing is a very abnormal and unhealthy relationship?" Or "Do you realize that what happened to you was a form of abuse?" It is not uncommon for such people to disagree, to minimize the hurt they received, and to defend their parents. To them, what they are describing is normal. It's all they've ever known.

Another related challenge I face as a counselor is getting people to see their own parenting style more objectively. They don't realize that the way they are parenting their own children is just as "out of whack" as what they grew up with. It may have taken a very different form. The child of a dictatorial and emotionally distant parent may become a Parent Who Loves Too Much. The child of unmotivated, nonachieving parents might become a compulsive ultraperfectionist and may impose these same obsessive expectations on her own children.

So my challenge to you is to examine yourself and your own parenting style carefully. Examine your assumptions about the family background you came from and the family environment you are providing for your children now. Remember that the deceptive power of denial is strong in all of us and often prevents us from seeing the truth about our own issues and our own behavior.

Then ask yourself, "Is there a cycle of abuse or neglect or enmeshment or control or perfectionism that I have inherited from my parents? Am I passing that cycle on as a hurtful legacy to my own children?" That cycle *can* be broken. *You* can break it. In the rest of this chapter, we will examine seven principles for breaking the cycle so that you can pass on an inheritance of love, security, and independence to your children. I call these principles:

THE SEVEN KEYS TO BREAKING THE CYCLE

KEY #1:
FOCUS ON YOUR OWN HEALING FIRST

Many parents subscribe to the mistaken notion that to be a good parent, you must deny your own needs and think only of the needs of your child. The truth is that to take care of your own needs and your own healing first is not an act of selfishness but an act of love for your children. To be emotionally healthy, kids need emotionally healthy parents.

In the Minirth-Meier Clinic book *Kids Who Carry Our Pain,* Dr. Robert Hemfelt and Dr. Paul Warren observe that when parents bring their children into the clinic for counseling, their order of priorities is usually inverted. "Almost invariably," they write:

1. Fix the kid who is messing up.
2. Well, okay, if you want to tinker around with the marriage a little, we suppose it won't hurt. Might do some good.
3. Fix me personally? I don't need fixing. It's the kid.

And absolutely without exception, the reverse is the correct order of priorities:

1. Heal thyself.
2. Work on the marriage.
3. Now help your children resolve their own problems without pressure from above. . . .

The best interests of the child are served better by far when the whole family makes constructive adjustments.[1]

Again and again, I've observed this same inversion of priorities as parents come into my office for counseling. They bring their "problem kid" in to be "fixed" by the psychologist. But "fixing" the "problem kid" is as futile as pumping up a tire with a leaky valve stem. The flat tire is only a symptom of a much more fundamental problem: the valve stem isn't working. Some families come into counseling and want to just keep pumping up the tire. They don't want to hear about the leaky valve stem in their family. "Just put some air in the tire," they say, "and we'll be on our way." But until they find and fix the root problem, the family tire will continue going flat.

I'm not saying that every time a child has an emotional problem, the parent is to blame. But I am saying that whenever a child has a problem, everyone in the family system partakes in that problem and has a role in implementing the solution to that problem. And very often that child's problem has a large part of its genesis in the emotional issues of one or both parents.

What can you do to find healing for yourself so that you can be a more healthy and helpful parent to your child? Here are some suggestions:

Reparent yourself to become a better parent. If you did not have healthy boundaries, unconditional acceptance, and continual validation of your God-given uniqueness when you were a child, you can be *reparented* and experience those nurturing benefits today. As you focus on receiving these emotional benefits in your own life, you will naturally become more conscious of the need to give these nurturing benefits to your own child.

As part of the reparenting process, accept God's validation of your own worth and uniqueness. If you did not receive this kind of validation as a child, allow God, your Heavenly Parent, to give you His validation. Many people seek their validation and self-worth from the praise of other people, from achievement and success, or from compulsively rescuing and subordinating themselves to others. But that kind of validation rarely satisfies because it is based on what we do. God accepts us not for what we do *but because of what he has done for us through Jesus Christ.* God does not accept us because of our achievements and our strengths. Instead, He freely accepts just as we are, in the midst of all our failures and our weakness. That is the kind of acceptance and validation you are really hungering for.

There are several steps you can take to receive the validation of God. First, meditate on the scriptural affirmations I've included in chapter 4, which are adapted from the book *Please Let Me Know You, God* by Dr. Larry Stephens (see pages 108–109). Second, read the Bible and pray daily, asking God to give you His peace, His love, and His validation through the Holy Spirit. Third, plug into a Christian support network—a support group, recovery group, or home fellowship Bible study through your church. The more we hear God's affirming voice speaking to us through the blended voices of His Word, His Spirit, and the unconditional affirmation of other Christians, the more secure we become and the greater our ability to convey a strong sense of security and validation to our own children.

Support groups and recovery groups are especially valuable to people who need validation and affirmation. Those groups become surrogate families; warm, secure environments for healthy reparenting. Unlike your family of origin, these surrogate families are built on a foundation of rules which foster healthy behavior, honest communication, and supportive encouragement. If there is ever criticism in a support group or recovery group, that criticism is constructive, caring, and humble, intended to build you up, not tear you down. Denial, abusive behavior, controlling behavior, manipulation, and deception are confronted in a caring way in these groups. The nonjudgmental atmosphere allows group members to drop their defenses, express their true feelings, and simply be themselves.

Organizations such as Alcoholics Anonymous, Al-Anon, Debtors Anonymous, Emotions Anonymous, Narcotics Anonymous, Overeaters Anonymous, and Incest Suriviors

Anonymous have chapters in virtually every major city in the country, offering programs built upon the foundation of the Twelve Steps (spiritual principles although not specifically Christian in nature). If you would prefer a Christian support group or recovery group, ask your local church, or contact Overcomer's Outreach and ask for the location of an Overcomer's group in your area. Write to Overcomer's Outreach at 2290 W. Whittier Blvd., Suite D, La Habra, CA 90631.

Give yourself permission to feel and express your emotions in a healthy way. If your parents taught you to seal off emotions, then you may be passing the same unhealthy messages on to your child. Find nondestructive ways to release your emotional energy (see chapter 6, pp. 107-112, for suggestions). Seek counseling for insight and help in dealing with your repressed emotions. As you learn to handle your emotions in a healthy way, you will find yourself giving your child the permission to feel and express emotions in a healthy way too.

Take on new challenges and healthy risks. Move outside yourself. Take the risk of trying new experiences, meeting new people, making new friends. Don't spend your life on a couch watching TV; expand your horizons and live life as an adventure. As you become more adventuresome, decisive, and independent, you will naturally begin to encourage these mature and independent qualities in your children.

Examine your inner reasons for parenting as you do. Counseling is a powerful tool for uncovering hidden issues and revealing deeply submerged motives for behavior. If you have difficulty understanding why you parent the way you do, use counseling to give you the insight and ability to become the parent you want to be.

If, for example, your parenting style creates enmeshment, find out why you tend to overparent. Is it because of emotional needs that were never met in your childhood? Is it because you have an unsatisfying marriage right now? Is it because some vague sense of guilt and inadequacy drives you to give and give to your child, far beyond his ability to receive? Perhaps you know you should release your child and let him live his own life, but you fear that letting go would create a vacuum in your life. Perhaps—like Deanna—you are overparenting with the idea that your enmeshed relationship with your child is actually a *great* relationship! Counseling can help to bring your issues into sharper focus so that you can create healthy boundaries, develop healthy relationships, and raise healthy kids.

If you are a driven parent who continually pushes your child into every extracurricular activity and who stands over your child during homework sessions, then counseling can help you understand the fears and insecurities which drive your behavior. For some reason, you are operating on a dangerous and destructive myth—the myth that unscheduled time is wasted time. Children are supposed to "waste time" just playing and running and exploring and daydreaming. That's their job.

One distributor of educational toys and games, Discovery Toys, has adopted this motto: "We believe that play is a child's work." That's a good motto for you to adopt as well, particularly if you are a driven parent raising driven kids. Don't feel you have to fill your child's time with activities and propel your child toward the stratosphere of accomplishments and awards. Let your child be a child. Let your child play. If you find that you are unable to keep from driving your child, then get professional counseling so that you can acquire the insights and skills you need to be the parent you want to be.

If you tend to be a controlling parent, you need to learn how to stop giving advice, how to stop obsessing and worrying over your child, how to stop imposing your will on your child, and how to focus on the positives instead of the negatives. Perhaps you think that if you don't help her and guide her decisions (in other words, *control her life*), she will fail and suffer. Counseling can help you understand how insecurities and fears about your own life cause you to dominate the lives of your children—and counseling can give you the understanding to help you to *stop*.

Whatever your parenting style, the most important step you can make in helping your child to be all he can be is for *you* to be all *you* can be. If you fix your own issues first, chances are your child's issues will begin to take care of themselves.

KEY #2:
MAKE YOUR MARRIAGE RELATIONSHIP A PRIORITY

Many people with seriously troubled marriages decide, "Well, I'll just write off or endure this bad marriage. I'll try to ignore this miserable person I'm married to and just focus on loving my children." Adopting such an attitude is a big mistake! Do you want your children to be emotionally healthy? Then remember this: one of the best things you can do to raise healthy children is to have a healthy marriage. Here are some suggestions for strengthening and repairing a sagging marriage:

Seek marriage counseling. If your partner won't go into counseling, then go alone (one partner in counseling is better than none). Talking to another person about the deep issues of your marriage relationship can be difficult at first, but it is a courageous first step toward healing and a real act of love for your children.

Make your marriage a priority. Set aside regular time to be alone with your spouse. Go out on a date. Do lunch or dinner, take in a movie or a show, take a trip, or just book a night in a hotel for a romantic rendezvous. Not only will it do your marriage a lot of good, but it will also do your child good to see her parents having fun together, enjoying each other's company, and building a relationship.

Commit yourselves to practicing open, honest, caring communication with each other. In effective communicating, words should match feelings, and behavior should match

words. Your goal should be speaking the truth and demonstrating love, not just winning an argument.

As you communicate with each other, make a commitment
to listen carefully, nonjudgmentally, and nondefensively. Try
to really hear what your spouse is saying; avoid projecting
your biases on your spouse or reading into her message or
mentally rehearsing your own speech while she is talking.
Reflect back what you hear to make sure you understand what
your spouse is really saying.

If you have needs that are not being met, communicate
them calmly and without blaming, then invite your spouse to
share his needs. Find out what is missing in the relationship,
and try to fill that gap.

Entertain the possibility that your spouse may have a legiti-
mate point even if your first impulse might be to argue the
point. At least suspend judgment and express that you would
be willing to think about it. Give up the right to always be
right.

*Draw appropriate boundaries in and around your marriage
relationship.* Keep a clear boundary around your marriage.
Make sure that extended family, friendships, work, and
church commitments do not intrude across that boundary.
Also, make sure that each of you has an appropriate boundary
around your own individual life. You need unity, but you also
need separateness. You each need your own goals, your own
interests, your own tastes, your own sense of self—and *all*
those facets of who you are need to mesh with who your
spouse is. But remember, they should *mesh*, not entwine. If
you and your spouse do not have a sense of your own unique
identities, you cannot come together in a healthy way.

Support each other in your parental roles. Confer together
on major decisions and agree together on your parenting
style. Avoid doing or saying anything that would undermine
your spouse's image or efforts as a parent. If you disagree
with your spouse, deal with the disagreement in private, not

in front of your children. Support and affirm your spouse as a person to be respected and obeyed as a parent.

Of course, many parents are facing the challenge of raising their kids without the support and help of a spouse. Single parents, don't lose heart. Being a divorced or widowed parent doesn't mean your children are doomed to become emotionally unhealthy. A single-parent home is not, by definition, a second-class family. You clearly have the power to make it a first-class family and to produce healthy, well-adjusted children. As a single parent, you can provide your children with everything they need: love, affirmation, validation, appropriate limits, healthy boundaries, and a secure sense of individuality and uniqueness. A two-parent family which is continually rocked by conflict is a much more unsettling and insecure environment for a child than a stable single-parent household. So don't worry. If you need some help coping with the challenges of parenting alone, join a single parents' support group or seek counseling. You and your children will likely do just fine.

KEY #3:
AFFIRM YOUR CHILD'S UNIQUENESS

If your own parents were enmeshed or dictatorial or controlling, then there is a good chance that vestiges of their parenting style will show up as you parent your children. You can overcome any unconscious tendencies to control your children by making a *conscious* effort to reinforce and affirm your child's uniqueness. All parents, from time to time, will praise or reward their children for "being just like Daddy" or "just like Mommy" in some way. Certainly, we want to be good models for our children. But we also want them to learn to think for themselves and to be comfortable with who they are as individual human beings, distinct from their parents.

What I am suggesting here is that to raise secure children, you must perform a delicate balancing act. On one hand, you want to pass on your values, the key elements of your faith, the joy of knowing a genuine relationship with God. But on the other hand, you want to encourage your child's independence, the ability to assemble her own picture of the world, and the courage to carve out her own unique place in it. Here are some suggestions for achieving this delicate balance:

Affirm aspects of your child that are unique and different from you. For example, you might say, "I'm very pleased to hear you have such a great singing voice. I was never much of a singer, but I love to listen to your music." Encourage your child to explore and uncover facets of himself which are unique and individual: interests, hobbies, skills, talents, gifts, ideas, and goals.

Affirm character qualities. Praising accomplishments can be good for a child's self-esteem—up to a point. But too much emphasis on achievement can make a high-achiever egotistical and narcissistic and can make a low-achiever feel inadequate and inept. A healthier approach to building a child up is to focus more on character qualities than on achievements. In Galatians 5:22–23, we find the most desirable and Christlike character qualities listed as "the fruit of the Spirit"; love, joy, peace, longsuffering (that is, patience and perseverance), kindness, goodness, faithfulness, gentleness and self-control.

You can always link accomplishments to a character quality and affirm that quality in your child. For example, if your child comes home with a good report card, try to focus as much or more on the character that produced those grades as on the grades themselves: "Those grades mean that you have really been conscientious and diligent and self-disciplined. They are a symbol of how hard you have worked. I'm really proud of you because of the kind of person you are becoming." A grade on a report card will be forgotten next week, but the strength of character your child is building will last a lifetime.

Avoid prophesying a future for your child, either positive or negative. "You'll never amount to anything!" It's clear to see the destructive power of those words. But in some cases it can be just as destructive to prophesy future glories or successes: "You're going to be a great preacher or evangelist someday!" Or "You're going to be a great leader someday, maybe even President!" Or "You're going to be a great writer!" Though well-intentioned and seemingly positive, such prophecies can be limiting to a child, forcing him to focus in one direction to the exclusion of all others. There is also evidence to indicate that one factor in producing narcissistic adults is a parent who prophesied grandiose dreams of the future. Instead of prophesying a future to your child, affirm your child's quest to discover the unique abilities, interests, gifts, and dreams God has given him.

KEY #4:
KEEP THE COMMUNICATION LINES OPEN

Your child is talking to you. She's excited, she's filled with enthusiasm, she's sharing something that is tremendously important to her. But all you hear is, "Yuh-duh yuh-duh yuh-duh *yaaaah*-yuh-duh yuh-duh!" Because you're thinking about something else. Or you're watching TV. Or you just don't think she has anything interesting or important to talk about. So you respond, at the appropriate points, "Uh-huh. . . . Oh, really? . . . That's nice, honey! . . . Now, go out and play!" You can fool a child for a while, but soon she figures out that she is not being listened to at all.

Children need to know they are important to their parents. When they feel they are not heard, they feel small and insignificant. And there are many other, more subtle ways we convey to our children that we aren't really hearing them. In a time of conflict, for example, we "listen" impatiently, tapping one foot and glaring while the child makes the case for his point of view, and as soon as he pauses for a breath, we pounce on him and prove him wrong!

Or we may try to control the child's message instead of really listening to what the child is saying: "You don't really feel that way." Or "That's a terrible thing to say." Or "That's silly, that's nonsense." In effect, we are projecting our adult feelings and perceptions onto our child rather than really listening to what the child is telling us. When we deny and disallow a child's true emotions, we teach that child that her feelings are unimportant or shameful, and we condition that child to seal off her emotions. Children feel and reason differently from adults, and we should learn to affirm, allow, and enjoy those differences.

Here are some suggestions to improve communication with your children:

Practice active listening. Get down on your child's level, look him in the eye, and really *listen*. Use nonverbal cues to show you are paying attention to what your child is sharing: nod enthusiastically, smile, show warm facial expressions. Ask questions and paraphrase back to your child what you have heard so that your child *knows* he is being understood.

Demonstrate empathy—even in times of conflict. Empathy doesn't mean agreeing, it just means understanding. You can empathize with your child even while you completely disagree and even while you are disciplining her. You don't lose or give up anything by saying, "I don't agree, but I do understand why you feel that way," or "I understand that you were under a lot of peer pressure, and it was a tough choice; but you made an unwise choice, and you'll have to take the consequences for that choice."

Make sure your words and your behavior match. Say what you mean and mean what you say. Don't send mixed messages. For example, don't say, "I'm not angry," when your facial expression, your tone of voice, and your body language are screaming in rage. Your words, your behavior, and your body language should always speak in unison.

Share your feelings honestly. Teach your children by example that feelings are nothing to be ashamed of. Honest expression of your feelings teaches your children to trust you with their feelings.

Use "I" statements rather than "you" statements. "I" statements convey personal responsibility. "You" statements assign blame. Compare the impact of these two statements:

- "You" statement: "*You* make me so mad! *You* never keep your promises!"
- "I" statement: "*I* feel very frustrated and disappointed when you break your promises to me."

When you build a habit of using "I" statements when talking to your children, you model to them the fact that every person in the family is responsible for his or her own feelings.

Don't use prayer for preaching. "Lord," we pray during family devotions, "please help these children to stop driving me crazy! Please help them to do what they are told!" It's good for children to recognize their own sins and faults and to confess them in prayer. But we should not confess our children's sins for them! Misusing prayer this way is a form of triangling communication, with God as the third-person go-between. If we want to convey a message to our children about their behavior, it is much healthier to communicate with them directly, openly, and honestly. Prayer is for talking to God.

Hold regular family summit meetings. Select a day that everyone can remember—perhaps the first of each month or every Sunday night—and make the family meeting a regular event. Connie's family has family devotions (about fifteen minutes of singing, Scripture reading, and prayer before bedtime) every Sunday night through Friday night. Saturday night is "Family Pow-Wow Night," which is reserved for discussion and a short closing prayer. "We don't have a set agenda," Connie explains. "We give everybody in the family, from the biggest to the smallest, a chance to bring up any concern, gripe, or idea. We use the pow-wows for everything from discussing family conflicts to planning a trip to Disneyland. We try to keep the atmosphere nonjudgmental and even fun, and we have a rule: No reprimanding during pow-wow. It's the place where we celebrate our joys and grieve our losses."

KEY #5:
ABSOLVE YOUR CHILD OF GUILT

For years, Christopher has carried a vivid, guilt-drenched memory inside him: "I was four years old, sitting in the back seat of my parent's car. This was in the late '50s, before seat-belts, and I was standing with my feet straddling that middle hump, the transmission hump, and I was leaning over the front seat. My dad was driving and my mom was in the front seat next to him, holding my baby brother in her arms. I had this brand new toy car that I was so proud of, and I reached out and shoved it in front of my dad's face while he was driving and said, 'Look at this, Dad! Vrooom!' He pushed it out of his face and started to yell at me, and then there was a squeal of brakes and *crash!* We hit another car in the intersection. My baby brother was thrown out of my mother's arms and killed.

"Well, our family never talked about that day, but I always grew up thinking I had caused the accident, that I had killed my little brother. I lived with that guilt for over forty years. But just a few weeks ago, I was talking with my dad about that day, and I told him how guilty I had felt all these years because of that accident. He looked at me kind of stunned and said, 'Chris, you didn't have anything to do with that accident. That was caused by a guy pulling out from a side street.' I told him what I remembered, and he said that it didn't happen that way at all!

"As Dad and I discussed it, we figured out that somehow I had taken two events from about the same time in my life and squished them together into one terrible, guilty memory. In one of those events, I had put a toy in front of my dad when he was driving, and he told me to get it away or I would cause

him to have a wreck, but there was no wreck. Then, in a totally separate and unrelated incident, my family was out driving, we had an accident, and my little brother was killed. But
by merging those two memories into one, I took all the blame
for my brother's death into myself, and I kept it buried there
all these years."

Christopher's experience is far from unusual. In fact, it is
quite common for a child to feel responsible for everything
bad that happens in the family, from accidents to arguments,
from someone dying to parents divorcing. Psychologists call
this *self-referential thinking,* and it is a normal way for children to think. It is common, for example, for a child to feel
that he is to blame when parents can't get along. If they separate and divorce, then the child reasons, "They couldn't stay
together because I was bad." The child will often resort to behavior intended to bring the parents together—creating problems at school, attention-getting, manipulation ("Daddy's
been real sad because you won't let him live at home
anymore")—all in the belief that he caused the breakup and
has the power to undo the breakup as well.

One of the most important things we can do to raise emotionally healthy children is to absolve them of guilt. Here are
some suggestions:

*Make your child aware of the boundaries between parent
and child responsibilities.* Tell your child, "I am the
grownup, and you are the child. You are not responsible for
the things I do. You are not responsible for my sadness; I
was crying about something that happened at work." Or
"You are not responsible for the divorce. Your mother and I
had problems getting along even before you were born."
Or "You are not responsible for your sister dying. She got very
sick, and she died, and sad things like that happen in
life." Or "You were not to blame for what your father did to
you. It was his responsibility as an adult to control his behavior."

Apologize. Recognize and admit it when you have been

wrong. Tell your child, "I used to tell you that you were bad, but I was wrong. You were always a very sweet and well-meaning child. I was the one with the problem, not you, and I'm sorry I hurt you so much." Or "I realize that you have a right to feel angry toward me. I treated you unfairly."

When you apologize to your child for wrongs you have done, you show her that you are aware that you make mistakes; you show her (and yourself) that you do not have to be perfect; and you model an example of the way you want your child to live.

KEY #6:
SET HEALTHY BOUNDARIES IN YOUR
RELATIONSHIP WITH YOUR CHILD

Perhaps your parents did not have healthy boundaries in their relationship with you. By consciously deciding to have a well-bounded relationship with your own children, you can take one more step toward breaking the cycle. Here are some suggestions:

Don't rely on your children to meet your emotional needs. Remember Deanna's relationship with her daughter? Deanna thought they had a great relationship because they were more like friends than mother and daughter. They did everything together, and Deanna even confided personal secrets to her daughter and sought her daughter's advice. Deanna was doing her daughter a serious emotional disservice. It is not a child's role to be a confidante, a counselor, a supporter, or a priest to us. We should never turn to our minor children for comfort when we are feeling lonely, afraid, sad, depressed, or angry. Instead, we should:

- Confide in a friend or in our spouse.
- Confide in our own parents.
- Confide in a counselor, pastor, deacon, or elder.
- Attend a support group or small group Bible study.

- Record our feelings in a journal.
- Pray.

You may feel better after unburdening yourself to your child, but your child will probably feel worse. And that is a violation of your responsibility as a parent.

Don't share information about marital or sexual issues with your children. Saddling a child with the worries and tensions of your marital issues and intimacies is a form of abuse. It creates enormous conflict, anxiety, and worry in your child. It may force your child into a clash of loyalties between you and your spouse. If you have a serious marital conflict that your child is aware of, your role is not to lean on your child for emotional support but to reassure your child that this is *not* your child's problem in any way.

Assure your child that you are okay. Your child needs to feel secure. That child invests almost all his sense of security in knowing that the parents are in control, are coping, are protecting, are optimistic about the future. If you convey to your child that you can't cope, that you may not survive a given situation, that you can't take care of yourself (much less anyone else), then your child's whole world becomes a very unstable, unsafe, unpredictable place.

When problems come, and it is clear to your child that you have been affected by those problems, you can say, "This is not an easy situation, but I can cope with it. Everything's under control, and we're going to be okay. Don't worry about it." Make an effort to be positive, optimistic, and proactive—both for your children's sake and for your own well-being.

KEY #7:
GIVE YOUR CHILD A HEALTHY BALANCE
OF LIMITS AND INDEPENDENCE

Many adult children of enmeshed or controlling parents perpetuate that unhealthy cycle by inhibiting their children's sense of independence and adequacy. "I'm just a careful parent," they say. "It's a dangerous world, and I'm protecting my child." But they are really controlling and smothering that child. You can test your own willingness to foster (or frustrate) your child's independence by answering the following questions:

- Have you ever discouraged your child from making friends?
- Do you limit your child's activities away from home more than other parents do?
- When your child is out of your sight or control, do you worry and feel anxious about her well-being?
- Have any of your friends or family members suggested to you that you might be an overprotective parent?
- Do you tend to involve yourself in your child's schoolwork, outside activities, friendships, and interests?
- Do you feel fearful, anxious, or depressed at the thought of someday having an "empty nest"?

A preponderance of yes answers to these questions indicates that you need to loosen the reigns of control over and involvement in your child's life. Here are some suggestions for becoming more conscious about giving your child the freedom to grow:

Encourage your child to have friendships of her own. You should not be your child's entire world. Your child needs to develop a growing sense of the society beyond her own four walls and a growing sense of independence. If your child wants to join a scouting organization or a church youth club, then encourage that interest. If your child wants to spend the night with a friend or go with a friend to Wild Water Park for the day, say yes. Encourage your child to enlarge her circle of friends and sphere of activities.

Practice letting your child do his own work. If your child doesn't get schoolwork done without your nagging, try stepping back. Let the child rise or fall on his own merits. Let him take responsibility for his own success or failure. Instead of nagging your child to get his chores done, tell him once; then impose appropriate consequences (such as the loss of a privilege) if the chore isn't done.

Seek counseling or a parents' support group for help in dealing with anxiety and worries. If you are terrified of the empty nest or if you find it extremely difficult to let your child spend the night with a friend, then you clearly have an issue which—if you fail to deal with it decisively—could create emotional and relational hindrances for your children. For your child's sake, get professional help and resolve those feelings.

GOOD ENOUGH PARENTS

"I knew I had a lot of bitterness toward my mother," Deanna says today. "Her intrusiveness, her controlling behavior, her continual criticism made me feel bad about myself and all churned up. But until I was in counseling, I didn't realize how much hurt I had suffered in so many areas of my life. My self-esteem was hammered right into the ground. My marriage suffered. My relationship with my sister suffered. And worst of all, by reacting so extremely against the way I was parented, I was doing harm to my own daughter.

"Now I have better boundaries in my relationship with my mother. I'm working on my compulsive behavior, especially my compulsive overeating. I'm in a support group for parents, and I feel the group is really helping me to be reparented by God. Most of all, I'm enjoying a new relationship with my daughter, a relationship with boundaries. That's been the hardest thing of all—learning to release my daughter, little by little, into the world. I don't like letting her go on field trips and to slumber parties with her friends, but I can't keep her like a bird in a cage. I can tell she's happier now, and deep down, despite the anxieties and fears I still have to resolve, I'm really happier too.

"One of the things I still have to do a lot of work on," Deanna concludes, "is the guilt I feel for some of the harmful things I've already said and done to my daughter. Everything else in my life was so imperfect, I thought that at least I was being the perfect parent, and then I found out I was even messing up *that* job! I've had a talk with my daughter, and I've told her it was wrong of me to confide in her my marital secrets, my suicidal thoughts, and other emotional issues. I don't think she fully understood why I was asking her forgiveness, but I wanted to make a clear boundary in our relationship that we both would be aware of. Someday I hope to look back and say, 'Maybe I wasn't such a bad parent after all.'"

Deanna is making progress. But there is one more crucial principle of parenting she needs to learn, internalize, and practice in order to break the cycle and become the kind of parent she truly wants to be. That principle is so simple, it can be stated in two words: *Just relax!* Try not to worry and obsess about being the perfect parent and raising perfect children. In their book *When Parents Love Too Much*, Laurie Ashner and Mitch Meyerson suggest that instead of striving for perfection, we should strive instead to be what they call "good enough parents." They write:

> Good enough parents provide for their children's needs without becoming enmeshed in every drama of their lives. They don't attempt to orchestrate their children's social lives, or fight battles for them. They encourage their child's internal strengths and qualities without becoming overly concerned with externals or the way their child compares with others. They provide a non-judgmental atmosphere in which self-esteem is fostered, without anxiously judging the child who can't live up to

rigid expectations. . . . They understand that making mistakes is a part of the learning process—even for parents. Most of all, good enough parents encourage the child's independence, realizing that the child's emotional separation from them is a healthy step to maturity.[2]

I agree. In my experience, perfect parents are *terrible* parents. Perfect parents raise the kind of children that create job security for psychologists and psychiatrists. If you want to break the cycle and avoid passing on a legacy of hurt, then whatever you do—*please don't be perfect!*

The best parent in the world is a parent who is just good enough.

In the next chapter, we conclude by answering the question so many people ask: "After all the turmoil I have been through, how can I forgive my parents, make peace with the past, and get on with my life?"

Making Peace with the Past

"**H**ow can I ever forget what my parents did to me?"
That's the question Jill asks. She is a Christian
in a very responsible position as the administrator of a
medium-sized health maintenance facility. From the time she
was a child, her accomplishments never pleased her parents,
no matter what she achieved, no matter how hard she tried. If
she got one B+ on an otherwise straight-A report card, she
was not allowed to watch television for two weeks. When she
graduated with honors from her university, her mother wept
because Jill wasn't the valedictorian.

Today, Jill is a driven career woman who feels guilty taking
any time out for recreation, relaxation, or social life. She
hates her drivenness but is gripped by a workaholic compulsion. She feels tremendous bitterness toward her parents and
refuses to speak to them. As a Christian, Jill feels she should
make peace with her parents, but she doesn't know how.

"My parents ruined my life! How can I ever forgive what
they did to me?"

Glynnis's father sexually abused her from the time she was
eight until she was in her teens. Glynnis is certain that her
mother knew about the abuse but did nothing to stop it. After
several years of counseling, she finally gathered the courage

to confront her parents, and both parents completely denied it ever happened, became hostile to the point of threatening her life, and then completely cut off all contact with her.

"What am I supposed to do with these people?" she asks. "Should I just try to forget them and go on? I don't think I can do that. But I can't forgive them and reconcile with them either. What other options are there? As far as I can see, it's catch-22."

"My father's dying. I need to forgive him, but I just can't. Pretty soon, it'll be too late for forgiveness."

The clock is ticking for Edward, a young pastor of a small congregation on the West Coast. Two years ago, his father—who is in his mid-fifties—suffered a succession of mysterious illnesses. Just recently, a diagnosis was finally rendered: Edward's father has a case of full-blown AIDS, the result of a secret homosexual lifestyle. Edward is devastated, and he is angry. He never imagined that his father might be carrying on a secret life.

Now Edward's father is blind, and his mind is deteriorating rapidly. His body is riddled with cancer, and he weighs only 110 pounds. The doctors predict he will live only a few more months at most.

"I feel I don't even know my father anymore," says Edward, "almost as if I have been robbed of my father and everything my childhood meant. How do I make peace with a man who has been lying to me all his life about who he really is? I don't know how to forgive him, but if I don't forgive him before he dies, can I ever forgive myself?"

What all of these people have in common is this agonizing question: "How do I make peace with my parents—and with the past?" Each of these individuals feels engulfed by painful memories, regret, guilt, shame, and bitterness. They want to know what it means to forgive and be forgiven; how to release old hurts and get on with their lives; how to fulfill God's command to honor parents despite a barrier of resentment and pain. Perhaps these are issues which haunt your own emotions and memories as well.

In this concluding chapter, we will examine together a practical strategy that will enable us to close the books on the past; live a rich, full life in the present; and face the future with courage, confidence, and hope.

THE POISON OF BITTERNESS

If there is one emotion that seems, more than any other, to afflict adult children of parents who were unloving, controlling, abusive, or enmeshed, that emotion would be *bitterness*. In my practice, I continually see people who are seething with bitterness toward their parents. Bitterness is the result of an attitude that says, "I have been deeply hurt, and I can never forgive that hurt. I will resent it as long as I live." This attitude poisons every dimension of our lives. It poisons our *spirits*, our *minds*, our *emotions*, our *bodies*, and our *relationships*.

Bitterness poisons the *spirit* by turning us against God. Again and again, I have observed that people who choose to remain bitter against their parents invariably aim their resentment at God as well. They question the goodness and the love of God. Their reasoning goes this way: "God supposedly loves me and knows what's best for me, yet look at the parents He provided for me! How could God have let this happen to me? He brought these miserable experiences into my life for evil, not for good. I hate my parents for what they did to me, and I hate God for bringing those parents into my life."

Bitterness poisons the *mind* by affecting our reason and distorting our thinking. We begin to interpret all the events in our lives through the distorted lens of embittered thinking. When some new trial or hurt comes into our lives, we think, "I knew it! God is just out to get me again!" If we think someone is slighting us or hurting us—even if the slight is minor or imagined—we interpret it as more of the same kind of treatment we have "always" received, and we fly into an unreasoning and irrational rage.

Bitterness poisons the *emotions* to the point where the mere mention of a person's name can trigger rage, fury, and a torrent of cursing. The memory of the wrong that was done to you can fester inside you for decades, and the sting of that memory remains as fresh today as it was ten, twenty, thirty years ago. Bitterness can permeate every corner of your memories and emotions until it becomes the central pillar of your personality, the character trait which defines you and which other people will remember you for, long after you are dead.

Bitterness poisons the *body* and makes you more susceptible to disease, fatigue, aging, and death. Research indicates that toxic emotions such as anger, resentment, and depression suppress the immune system, increase the body's production of stress hormones, and increase the risk of high blood pressure, peptic ulcers, heart attacks, and strokes. When bitterness seeps into the body, it often requires a surgeon to cut it out.

Bitterness poisons *relationships* as bitter people spread their poisonous thoughts and feelings to the people around them. Bitter people frequently form alliances against other people in order to punish them and get revenge. Bitter people color the perceptions of other people with their angry perspectives. One bitter person has the power to infect and destroy an entire family, an entire business, an entire church. I've seen it happen many times.

THE ANTIDOTE TO THE POISON OF
BITTERNESS: FORGIVENESS

Forgiveness is a widely misunderstood concept. Indeed, Dr. Susan Forward, in her otherwise excellent book *Toxic Parents,* includes a chapter called "You Don't Have to Forgive." Given her definition of forgiveness—"giving up the need for revenge, and absolving the guilty party of responsibility"—I am not surprised that she feels that forgiveness "could actually *impede* [the emotional healing] process rather than *enhance* it."[1] But Dr. Forward's definition is not the Bible's definition of forgiveness.

From a biblical perspective, forgiveness does indeed mean giving up the desire for revenge, but it emphatically does *not* mean absolving guilty people of their responsibility! That would be like saying down is up or sin equals righteousness. It would mean that forgiveness is an act of unrealistic thinking bordering on insanity! Authentic Christian forgiveness looks the reality of sin right in the eye without flinching, and it speaks the truth. It calls abuse, violation, and mistreatment by their proper names.

The prototype of forgiveness in the Bible is the story of Joseph in the book of Genesis. You probably know the story. Joseph's brothers became jealous of him and were going to kill him. Then one of the brothers said, "Wait, we can get rid of Joseph and make a profit to boot!" So they sold their brother into slavery in Egypt. There he rose to become the top slave in his master's household. But then the boss's wife took a shine to him and tried to seduce him, and when he wouldn't yield to her advances, she accused him of rape (one of the earliest cases of sexual harassment on record). Joseph went to jail. It seemed that the more exemplary and righteous his behavior, the worse he was treated.

Finally, in a surprise reversal of his fortunes, Joseph was elevated to the post of prime minister of all Egypt, second in power only to Pharaoh. And that's when he again encountered his brothers. They had come to Egypt during a time of famine, giving Joseph a perfect opportunity to take revenge. He had the power to punish, even destroy, his brothers. But he didn't. Instead, he forgave them. And in the process of forgiving his brothers, he gave us a principle that serves as an excellent guide to the true nature of Christian forgiveness. This principle has come to be called "The 50:20 Prin-

ciple" because it is found in Genesis 50:20. There, Joseph
says, "You meant evil against me; but God meant it for
good."

In these words of Joseph we find a component of forgiveness that Dr. Forward and so many other people miss: forgiveness does not excuse abuse or pretend that an abuser was not
responsible for his actions. Joseph says, in effect, "What you
did to me was wrong, it was evil, and I'm not excusing your
abuse. But God was able to use even that to bring about good
in my life and the lives of many other people."

Christian forgiveness recognizes that God can take all the
hurt and garbage this world heaps upon us, and He can recy-
cle it into a foundation to build a beautiful new life upon. If
that sounds like nonsense to you right now, then let me tell
you a story.

A HORROR STORY

Roger came to me for counseling once a week for three
months before I found out why he was coming. Every week,
Roger brought a friend from his church to sit in my office with
him because Roger had no capacity for trusting people, not
even a counselor. Something had happened in his life that
had left him so distrustful that he couldn't bring himself to
tell his story. After three months of talking superficially about
his job and his church and movies he had seen, Roger finally
began to open up a little about his past. His story came out in
bits and fragments over an agonizingly long time. And no
wonder. It was a horror story beyond anything Stephen King
ever imagined.

Roger's parents were members of a Satanic cult. His father
was a drifter and his mother was a prostitute. Throughout his
childhood, Roger and his two sisters were ritually, sexually,
and physically abused, and forced to participate in horrible
occult rites. As a teenager, Roger was forced into homosexual
prostitution to provide drug money for his parents. I will

spare you the lurid details; it's enough to know that he survived an ordeal of unimaginable terror and pain.

After he was old enough to escape his parents' domination, Roger was befriended by a Christian young man he met at work. Through this friendship, Roger became a Christian. As he studied the Bible, Roger became convicted about the fifth commandment: "Honor your father and mother." Did that mean that he had to honor these abusive, devil-worshiping monsters who had raised him? What sort of honor could he possibly owe them? And should he forgive them? Should he pretend that the ritualized violence and sexual horrors of his childhood never happened? And what about the rest of his life? How could he possibly lead a normal life and experience normal relationships after everything he had been through?

These were the questions Roger brought into my counseling office, and we dealt with those questions one by one. He had entered counseling with the belief that his life had been ruined by his parents. But as we talked together and explored his issues, he came to see his life from a new perspective. With each added insight, a new perspective began to dawn: *the events in Roger's life which had caused him so much pain and shame had also made him stronger.*

He is a survivor. He is a resilient, street-smart, courageous young man. He has a clear sense of his own identity and a strong, tenacious will. He won't ever let anyone use and exploit him again. He is extraordinarily sensitive. He can spot a phony in a flash. In fact, if I ever wanted to get a quick, reliable assessment of another person's character, I would have Roger sit down and chat with that person for a few minutes. He has an intuitive gift for sizing up other people, a gift he developed from early life as a survival technique.

I sometimes wonder if Roger would have all of these strengths if not for the painful experiences in his life. This does not mean that what his parents did to him was good. But it does mean that God can take all the nonsense in our lives and make sense out of it—*if* . . .

And this is a big *if* . . .

If we are willing to turn our pain and brokenness over to Him. *If* we are willing to respond to our pain in a Christlike way. *If* we are willing to forgive.

I've seen many people go through their lives clutching anger, resentment, and hatred to themselves because of the parents God has given them—and those people's parents were Ward and June Cleaver compared with the parents who raised Roger! These poor, embittered souls who make a choice to reject the love and goodness of God will go to their graves with bitterness and hate oozing from every pore.

But there are also people like Roger who, after working through their issues and their memories, make a joyous discovery: God has used the grief and pain of their lives to build them into better, stronger, kinder, more resilient people. And as they make this discovery, the questions that brought these people into counseling begin to be answered:

How, biblically, am I to honor people who have hurt me, abused me, and damaged me emotionally? I can honor them by respecting them for who God made them to be in my life. I don't have to like them or be friends with them or reconcile with them. But I can respect their role in my life as my God-given parents. God wasn't pleased by what they did, but He wasn't surprised either. God knew who our parents would be, and He still gave them to us. That is why we honor them and respect them.

How do I pretend that the abuse and the mistreatment never happened? I don't. I acknowledge that pain as a fact—and I learn and grow from it. I turn it over to God and ask him to transform it into Christlike character that can benefit me and the people around me.

What about the rest of my life? How can I lead a normal life after the hurt I've suffered? By forgiving those who have hurt me. By letting go of my desire for revenge. By letting go of my bitterness. By recognizing that, even though my parents may have meant it for evil in my life, God can use even that pain for good.

Every person I've counseled who has truly adopted this attitude, who was willing to forgive, who was willing to allow God to transform past hurt into present healing, has gotten better. Every single person, without exception. I've seen God take the adult children of parents who prophesied, "You'll never amount to anything" and turn them into people who overcame their compulsions and drivenness, people who strive for excellence in a healthy, balanced way. I've seen God take the adult children of unloving, narcissistic parents and turn them into people who were very caring and sensitive to the needs of other unloved people. In each case, just as David wrote in Psalm 56:8, God has taken the tears of these people and put them in His bottle, and when that bottle was again uncorked, those tears had been transformed into fragrant, satisfying wine.

HOW DOES FORGIVENESS WORK?

At this point, the idea of forgiveness may be starting to make sense to you. But now you want to know, "How do I get started? How does forgiveness work? What's the first step I need to take in order to forgive?" Let's look at the practical mechanics of forgiveness.

Forgiveness is a choice, not a feeling. And that's great news. If you have been emotionally wounded by your parents, you probably don't *feel* like forgiving them. Forgiveness is not an emotional experience; it's a choice and an action—a very practical action.

Forgiveness is unilateral. Your decision to forgive does not depend on anyone else's actions. You don't have to wait for your parents to change or repent or apologize. You can forgive them right now, even if they choose to remain monsters. Forgiveness is something which is totally in your power.

Your ability to forgive is rooted in a new perspective on the person who hurt you. You need to see that abusive or controlling parent in a new way. You need to see her through God's eyes, instead of through the small, scared eyes of a wounded child. When you see that parent through God's eyes, she no longer looks so big and scary. That bullying or abusive parent is really an insecure person filled with pain and fear.

When God calls you to forgive this person, He says, "Forgive your parent as I have forgiven you. I have sent Jesus to earth to take your sin and pain and bitterness onto Himself, and through His death and resurrection, I have wiped it all away. I did not have to send Jesus to lift you out of your sin, but I did. I loved you and forgave you unconditionally. Now I ask you to do the same for your parent."

In Matthew 18, Jesus tells the story of a servant who owed a great debt to his master. The servant pleaded for mercy, and the master forgave the debt. Later, however, this same servant accosted one of his fellow servants, who owed him a small debt. When the fellow servant pleaded for mercy, the servant who had been forgiven hardened his heart and threw the fellow servant into prison. To put ourselves into that story, it's as if God had forgiven the million-dollar debt we owed him, and we went out and threw our parents in jail because they owed us ten bucks. God says to us, "I've forgiven you so much—now it's your turn to forgive."

You can argue with that analogy. You can say your parents have dealt out a good deal more than ten bucks worth of misery to you, and I won't argue the percentages with you. I will say only this: God has forgiven you, and now he expects you to look at others, including your parents, from His perspective. And He urges you to forgive.

When you forgive, you acknowledge that you are on the same plane with the person who hurt you. You are no better than your parent. Every person in the world stands in need of God's grace and God's forgiveness. That is God's perspective.

Forgiveness is not just something you do for others; it is even more importantly something you do for yourself. When you harbor bitterness and unforgiveness toward your parents, you continue to allow them to victimize you. You allow them to sit in the driver's seat of your emotions. You remain emotionally bound to your parents by your own resentment and hatred. When you forgive your parents, you actually free yourself from their control. You remove them from the driver's seat, so they no longer occupy such an important place in your feelings and your behavior.

Forgiveness breaks the cycle of pain and blame. I have seen it take place over and over. Two stubborn people square off against each other, each insisting, "I'm right! You're wrong! You admit it and apologize, and *then* I'll forgive you!" Neither party will back down or even budge. But if just one of those people would choose forgiveness, the cycle of pain and blame will be broken. Forgiveness doesn't answer the question of who was right or wrong, of whose cause was just, or who started it, of who should take what percentage of the blame. But forgiveness allows hurting relationships to start over with a clean slate.

I've seen many people make an incomplete job of forgiveness. They say, "I'll forgive you—as soon as you've suffered enough." Or "I'll forgive you—just this once." Or "I'll forgive you—as soon as you apologize." True Christlike forgiveness is final. It is complete. It is unconditional. And it erases blame.

Forgiveness doesn't necessarily mean reconciliation. Forgiving your parents doesn't necessarily mean you are going to have a new relationship with them. They may not understand or want your forgiveness. They may not care whether you forgive them or not. They may not apologize or repent. They may continue being just as evil and abusive as ever; in fact, if you tell them you forgive them, they may become twice as abusive and hostile as before. You may not know where to find your parents, or they may even be dead. None of that matters. You can still forgive for the sake of your own emotional and spiritual well-being. It doesn't mean you've forgotten or excused what they did to you. It just means that you have released the past.

Our response to our parents can be like the response of Joseph to his abusive brothers: "You meant evil against me: but God meant it for good." We can say, "I'm not responsible for what my parents did to me. I'm only responsible for what I do now. I can either settle into the victim role for the rest of my life, or I can choose my own attitude and step out of the victim role. And the attitude I choose is an attitude of forgiveness. Though my parents may have meant it for evil, God can use all the circumstances of my life for good, both His good and mine."

Forgiveness is a process. Forgiveness isn't something you do once and for all. The fact that you forgive an event in your life does not mean it is suddenly wiped out of your memory. Anger and pain will come back to you again and again, and each time those feelings return, you will have to forgive again. But each time you forgive, you will repattern your thinking and rechannel your feelings just a little bit more. Eventually a time will come when the old memories and emotions will no longer return. They will be a thing of the past. The task of forgiving those hurts will finally be complete, and you will be at peace.

PEACE!

Scott's father abandoned him and his mother when Scott was only ten years old. Scott saw his father only two times after that, and on those two occasions, his conversations with his father were brief and laced with bitterness. Then when Scott was eighteen years old, word reached him that his father had died, leaving him a considerable amount of money in his will.

But there was a catch.

The will stipulated that the inheritance would go to Scott if and only if he agreed that once each year he would go to the town where his father was buried, kneel at his father's grave, and spend three hours praying for his father's soul.

At first, Scott was so glad to receive the inheritance that he thought nothing of fulfilling this provision in the will. But after five or six years of this, the thought of having to carry out the wishes of his dead father—a man who had abandoned him and his mother—began to gnaw at him. Each year he went to that cemetery to pray, he resented it more. Eventually it became almost impossible to carry out his father's wishes: How can you spend three hours on your knees praying for a man you hate?

"It got to the point," Scott recalls, "that I would have intense feelings of anxiety, along with physical symptoms such as digestive problems and heart palpitations. I dreaded the annual trip to that cemetery more than I ever dreaded anything in my life. I hated that old man, I hated his money, I hated the life-style I had purchased at the price of annual bondage to a dead man's will.

"That's why I went into counseling, and that's how I learned to forgive and make peace with my father. It wasn't easy. It still isn't easy. But I made a decision to forgive him, and I'm sticking to that decision. There were times over the past few years when I was absolutely convinced that the old guy gave me all that money just to torment me. I actually believed he had some kind of crystal ball, and he could see the hell he was putting me through by making that stipulation in his will.

"But now I realize that, even though he imposed a terrible burden on me, he was really trying to say, 'Son, I love you. I'm sorry I abandoned you. I never got to have a relationship with you while I was alive—maybe we can have this pseudo-relationship after I'm gone. Please, just pray for my soul once a year, okay?'

"So I do it. I don't know if it does my father any good. But I think it does me some good. If it hadn't been for this weird provision in my father's will, I don't think I ever would have learned how to forgive and make peace with the past. There's no feeling in the world like peace."

Scott is right. There is nothing in the world like knowing real peace.

The past is past. The future lies before you. Take it and live it as a strong, independent adult. You are free to be your own person, free to love, free to forgive, free to make peace with the people who raised you, free to truly *live*.

I wish you peace—God's perfect peace—as you continue your journey toward wholeness.

Notes

Chapter 1: Honor Your Father and Your Mother
1. Exodus 20:12.

Chapter 2: Why the Family?
1. John 8:32.

Chapter 4: Too Much Love or Too Little Love?
1. M. Scott Peck, *People of the Lie* (New York: Simon and Schuster, 1983), p. 75.

Chapter 5: Parenting Styles That Hinder Healthy Relationships
1. 1 Chronicles 4:9–10.
2. See Genesis 2:19.
3. See Genesis 35:18.

Chapter 6: Abusive and Seductive Parents
1. Proverbs 26:18–19.
2. Psalm 23:4.
3. Mark 10:14.
4. Larry Stephens, *Please Let Me Know You, God* (Nashville: Thomas Nelson Publishers, 1993), pp. 58–59.

Chapter 8: How to *Really* Love a Parent

1. Harold H. Bloomfield, M.D., with Leonard Felder, Ph.D., *Making Peace with Your Parents* (New York: Ballantine, 1983), pp. 4–8.

Chapter 10: "Gray Areas"—The Special Problems of Aging Parents

1. Matthew 5:4.
2. Isaiah 46:4.
3. Ambassador radio broadcast, "Dad—The Tender Warrior," Father's Day, June 20, 1993 (Ambassador Advertising Agency, 515 E. Commonwealth Ave., Fullerton, CA 92632; 714-738-1501).

Chapter 11: Breaking the Cycle

1. Robert Hemfelt and Paul Warren, *Kids Who Carry Our Pain* (Nashville: Thomas Nelson Publishers, 1990), pp. 139–140.
2. Laurie Ashner and Mitch Meyerson, *When Parents Love Too Much* (New York: Avon Books, 1990), p. 285.

Chapter 12: Making Peace with the Past

1. Susan Forward, *Toxic Parents: Overcoming Their Hurtful Legacy and Reclaiming Your Life* (New York: Bantam Books, 1990), p. 186.